The Wild Hunt Divinations

Trevor Ketner

# THE WILD HUNT

[Wesleyan Poetry]

# DIVINATIONS

*a grimoire*

Wesleyan University Press · Middletown, Connecticut

Wesleyan University Press

Middletown CT 06459

www.wesleyan.edu/wespress

© 2023 Trevor Ketner

Manufactured in the United States of America

Typeset in Parkinson Electra by Eric M. Brooks


Library of Congress Cataloging-in-Publication Data

available at https://catalog.loc.gov/

cloth: ISBN 978-0-8195-0038-0

paper: ISBN 978-0-8195-0039-7

e-book: ISBN 978-0-8195-0040-3


5  4  3  2  1

The Sonnets are different from *Leaves of Grass* in that their popularization, never mind their popularization as homosexual documents, did not occur until centuries had detached them from their original social, erotic, and narrative contexts. The tradition of the Sonnets is the tradition of reading them plucked from history and, indeed, from factual grounding.

Eve Kosofsky Sedgwick,
"Swan in Love: The Example of Shakespeare's Sonnets"


Deliberate breaking and shrinking both render objects unusable and therefore serve to remove them from the world of the mundane, thus symbolically "killing" them (much as happens with an animal or human sacrifice). The objects are thus transformed in order to enable their reception by the gods.

Miranda Aldhouse-Green,
*Sacred Britannia: The Gods and Rituals of Roman Britain*


What strong neck, what bright eye. What menagerie
we are. What we've made ourselves.

Donika Kelly,
"Love Poem: Chimera," in *Bestiary*

# Contents

## [From fairest creatures we desire increase,]

recites desire: runic frame / seas of trees—*raw*
*bead* rhymes *their teeth*—bone tug, ivy tear—
chamber *he* beauteously / dress it tepid
to see *they* shimmer, hiding *her* / ram rib
tits—heterocountry hag / bitchwood tune bent
weightless—us: fun filth / flat amethyst battlefields—
i am manic, naked, answerable—feign hue
(too yellow cyst / housefly thefts)—tree heft
warms heart—wrathful thorn neons to dot the
god or ash—tin daughter, lend any ply
bow; bend it to hunt—(hit)—new, synthetic ruin—
(sung) *a drinking stag wreathed in tender calm*—
brittle pewter, holy stone, i gold shut
and throw these teeth—a duet—gravel—boyed.


## [When forty winters shall besiege thy brow]

gowns web (herb hysteria)—let's thin flowery
then—gaudy bicep—insistent herd—leaf dyed
to holy doorway—hunt syrups—doze—given
that i swallow debt, let me whorl—feed lard
/ ale / ill breath—they get eye winks—husband,
of thudhurt, eyeray, saltwar—sheets yell,
*tan*—nude hyphen—i knot woe; sinewy, it sees
fingernails (limp waters, a hand sea), leather sets,
he-messes—hewed out virus—debauchery: try a mop
or a match—i hot—i lucid—i wonderflush—*stiffens*:
exoskeleton / cum—my cuddly human mass—*la*,
sings a boyish brute in his coven—cut—yep,
hood him—we want a wren duet, to be shelter—
a cold thud (trans sob / melt)—oh welt / honeyed wife.

## [Look in thy glass and tell the face thou viewest,]

synthetic floodgate: elk howl—unleash vase / tit
(oh art)—to witness that macho hem i ruffled one—
sewn, i warp, woof, hunt, (re)forest—shine, oh, tree,
lush in mothered mood / trowel's glut—see south ebb:
swish of brood, rare ewe whine, farmhouses—
ghostly fish head—daily i start / unbend—
white floweriness (blob)—moth / hood /
footsy—the silver of *slit* (top pose)—
hetero man he-thirst—stags' holy sundeath—
lovably lip them-holes, reap arc flicker—
i hound—oh i set to hug hole's fearless thaw—gown
(foreskin), let me get dishonest: i ply width,
i mouth orb, i meet bone—*verb* led *tuft*
inside—i heat—a sweetening middle height.


## [Unthrifty loveliness, why dost thou spend]

fleshy stud / nip void—holy hurts went stone,
lacy, petty—they bang—you flesh us
—(stun)—another ghost bed—(sung)—i vent / bled quiet—
able transfer / kindness gene / hoofed heart—
sub gushes a hydra / a bone note duet—tug it how
i have—teethe, beg, volunteer—i gut songs so
they sour—lush furs, sir, sewed up—*to to*
(a soft stammer, it nags us)—coven lets you
leaf fern—*froth, filth, caving*; say it—who
wove the ode; testify—soft chests, fully heed
teeth—echo a whole glen—neon hewn at burst:
sit / watch nova—ache at a deep cut—ate bull /
thumbed amethyst hunt bud—you bite sweet /
lush, witches—i doe, hex, butter, cove.

## [Those hours that with gentle work did frame]

kneed the ghost softer (*i hurt*)—draw with loam—
the reedy gazelle wove her vow—they yelled /
ate me—shy, i try valley, wept saltthorn—
hard wet chiffon / latex, a lacy hurt—hind,
*in (re)forming i elm*—severs meat: rots—nude
case for hedonism: deer in hunt—hit to wound
(*he* vow)—statuesque delinquents shred fog—a clay tip—
a strawberry—head (eyebrow seed)—even nouns
tire—metal tit / sin helmet—no furled snows—
no sprawled frills—a lisp—a questioning—
eyeteeth wet by a sweatier ebb—cuff turf:
name it *marrowbone, cairn, wet thorns*—
met otter (wine)—i fold twilights: dewy hush / belt hurt
hues—seers slit / etch bi violetswell—he wants bitter use.

## [Then let not winter's ragged hand deface]

i tang / tend gelded ache—trees thorn / fawn
home—test nihilist deer—rude blue myth /
amateur ass movie (peels lace hem)—stoke our wet
butterfly tissue—lithe, i beer / lard—a week's
fortunes (duds)—hosiery—taut nib—
peach pit whiplash—that lilyhag note—one wish:
to be feathers—dons hot fatherly tether—
form shinbone into petite pear tree—
in here, amethyst / a prophet rite (few hunt salt)—
i feint / fume—i set tender—there in the fog
hoofspells (*thud, thud, thud*), a coat widened—throat
thieving oval nips—i leg eternity—
i mold a funereal tit / frothblush crowfoot—
thin doe, *i breech dawn*—queer mass knots the atom.

## [Lo, in the orient when the gracious light]

oh, i gush it wet—oh enthralling erection
finished in cubly hug—desperate ash rune
—he-hag mishap / woodgrain night—steep to
hymn wrists—gloved kiss—ice—oh, jar tea,
spill—nymph deactivated *he*—hebull vinehang—
rib segment (roughed in)—a moss-tinged hilly
lull—oystered sky soot—*ah*—i omit tear—lab
(gold)—girls (indigo) eat inept men / hang
a sign: we froth butch carmyth—*hi, worm*—*hi, wept*—
heartbreak, feed me—eel-elegy of he-hilt
/ ewe-hoof—trees eat deus—try coven or dune:
a twin foothold—star—hemlock—any arrow—
i thigh stony, noon (tenuously)—hot fog—
lashes to lounge / out-do—to ink sun's end.


## [Music to hear, why hear'st thou music sadly?]

lay hum or hue—domesticity casts raw hush—
we try joint / joyless stones, whitewashed twig,
toy twitch—clove thaws the hour—i goldvest—unhealthy,
i set ulcer / intense rose wreath—naïve he-poly—
fecund fount / cold deli—*nowhere* rusts to
*here*—unbidden, it is a monday—roof fern /
housewife honeydew—etch clot (oddest hunt) by
hustling it—burns hart teeth—a shapeless son dot (
wideness) / woman-son—unhook hart—get herb tart
in the mouth—a dry bar rag (suck scene)—i lie /
i lie more (nymphs branch)—i'd gander pelt / dash
(a long, neon one)—i pond, so i heat (swelling)—
hygiene: no glob seen, no peach mess (swigs semen)—
lush net: girl(ish) tit photo—venison gone sweet.

## [Is it for fear to wet a widow's eye]

woof, await, destroy—i wife trees—
i salt / flesh tune (fish teem)—to sing *cunt* / holy
oath, i sea, i dust (lathes hiss hopeful)—
*wife* all white milkweed / tall ash—i wore sleek /
wildwild (howl twins)—yellow taper—the bed
has teeth—neon thudbolt—i froth foam heft—
i pile—needlework waver—why empty wave /
eyelash archery's hush pins—bends mind in bed
(dawn hunt)—told *worship*: oh, nettle; oh, fat rind—
water(shifted)color—filth splits (blush)—joy set in
bath habit / a nude want—end hurt, sweetly so—
top's honey tea—deerskins (sutured)—stud
-thirst—wooden moth / violet boar—ass (tons)—
macho cumthrust—*us*: mist, flesh omen, a dim shore.

## [For shame deny that thou bear'st love to any,]

*verb* so *a rhymed hunt*—a honey tool / fat taste
of toy—oh, welt (shiverpond)—trans fur—
(any loud boot) *that hurt*—finger wove flit (am
in them)—love note to unvast us both—i'd test
heat: piss hours to dust / us-weather (odors form)—
ghostly knot / stitch—i turn a peach(stone)—soft tits
(unhooks to see)—eat a fruit out, rig-beaten—
rode hitachi (flushed)—i brew hysteric hope /
honey cage—candy a moth—*am hung* / *tight* (myth)—hit
hole / oval den (feather, ball, straightened leg)—
i bend, sing, suck a seed—(sore) *i can't*—harpy,
hold; otter, rest—*okay*—heavens drift—a pelt
/ foam skeleton for them—heave or feel
it—a bull, teeth, ivythorn, an eye—i them—i salt.

[5]

## [As fast as thou shalt wane so fast thou growest—]

a sun shaft wets to lust—woofers ashoath a stag
photo—winter hunt: *hi* (an echo off)—at rest, i'd *them*
in frothy ballgown—boysect so wet—a hot (hushed) thud—
holy unwomanly hair tuft / scent—covehurt / smooth teeth—
a belt yearn (aroused, divine)—sinews chime
(low signal / fatty cud decoy)—i hold heat
/ odd mate: he howls; i fluster (dim silence / ease)—
aroma cults (they hoard away dew, red woe kernel,
a thousand warm moonteeth)—tether her so—loft
a shard—sees hairy deer pull ferns, burn earth—
more bookshelves: how we ghosted death—men
hold bows (tiny hecrush)—i hunt gush—i bounce out hot fits—
leather seams bend / rye / froth—arched net heave—
spit into the stud mouth—hold (porn)—*lace* yet *rot.*


## [When I do count the clock that tells the time,]

*cute hill* met *chest* (i held wheat / cotton knot)—
beaus and heavies—hunk (destroyed)—hinting
*them*—inhabit two poles (levered hip)—
dull screw (low drive)—inhale is saltbreath—
i see sweeter valleys—eat fob / horn / fern—
we froth dads (oh, they drip chains)—retch me
/ edge me—sun drums vale—i'd sing ear shrapnel
to brew tits—we hind / heron / bear—bed a rib thinly—
i *they*—i *dyke,* too—*me*: banquet of haunts—
am themgamut / soot to thaw gut—on fetishes:
see me devastate—looks unwind chest as fire / bees—
hetero ass is (*yawns*)—got sad / feathered—
fine neck edge candying a smitten stomach—hasten
he-hew (*he* knives the vertebra [ache teem])—a sob den.

## [O, that you were yourself, but love you are]

everywhere you auto to *boy*—a foul luster,
a silvery green hour (no fur to honey)—you sell
a promiscuous gay pelt—rend sight, a hind, one
moonseed—saw tiny beast leg over me—*rut*: echo
hunt—a toe lushes—holy boyish thaw / a lucid doe—
edenhoney / tin moon in tidewater—fur
(grayness)—fractured leaf / eye—i foul oases /
worry the forest—use swishy wound—use me (beau-role)—
sea, cutoffs, wood hysteria: all a hole—
hold dry, human hour with phonic bushing
(drag gown testament)—satisfy us, history /
carnal algebra—herd of otters and need—
bounty found: homo vein, true rye stalk, now
you—yes, stone (oh, rust), a foal, a hydra.


## [Not from the stars do I my judgment pluck,]

*form*: groped junk, mold taint, smut scythe—
noisemaker / vanity hymn—host date
(dull cub; foot overkill)—gotten too
grotesque / playful (shies so soon)—a draft / a
neon flutter cult—bone resin air motif—
i renounce it (hair, din, hand)—night tops dawn
(lilac flag)—i whip (it sews sorely)—north
bent / hidden—captivity (in / off earth)—
field me—work tight buds, rye omen, vine—eye
scam (trash tan trend)—hand resuscitation /
herb death (shatter)—*vanity*: total gush / lure
of wrist, mouth, tuft—do sore nerve cloth softly—
poetic holing fees—retro shit—to sea
(do stand by / taste)—i am houndsteady, huntred.

## [When I consider every thing that grows]

gathering thorn, sew *he* snowy—vice: dirt
  / nestcomfort—paint bound hill (let me tie),
bright teeth, stones—hunts ash to weepgush—taught
echo to lace—we rent unfit shrines—men crest men
(hip, harp, seacalm)—we cave-in (nest, entire nest)—
tender feed (he-squelch)—envy beaks / mesh / decay—
red vultures eat age—if i hunt, i hatch pantyhose—
meat shadow (our fatty reverb)—i tore name
to fit (hatchet)—stone, icy stone—scan ninth
sun (oh boyfemurs)—*ghost* yet *rot*, i mystic / i *he* (
safety died)—wheat me, blue weather twitch—
unaesthetic orgy (tough oily thud; no ado)—fly
me to the roof—raw, awful vinyl—*i, an idol,*
*foam you new*—untie a hare (forgets sky).


## [But wherefore do not you a mightier way]

a wood whim / fur ruby—eyeteeth: a rooting—
you, *wetter land marks it by moon at hip*—
*fairy*, not *furry*—deify doe lunacy so
she embers—braid my he-horns—my welt a remnant—
sunday top hunt—oh we spay hot—no proof
needed—snug asymmetry—a tannin ad (
wine, obviously)—i hew fowl's whirl / virtuous rut—drag
(in helmet; horror)—cute unpunk—i cite fat day
to eat fire—lush hole / a fir tip—holiness fled
to limp, runic nipple / mystic hip—he hews
wood (water ruin, water rind)—thin, fair horn—
inky sea full of *no*—use eye in memory cave
(a sly toil)—fur's wet, silver elegy—you speak of
bewilderments—you work lust / ivy land—you swan.

## [Who will believe my verse in time to come]

lilies move woe—convert: eye him-limb (wet
him if wifely)—dress is (tug it) the other world—
a sob mouth / knottiness but a heavy weight
has lifted—at prissy hour you wolf / chew hard on shin—
you watercolor (defy yet bite hue)—if us, *i*
means *hurry*—i means *go burn sacred bull* / *fern* /
*dogtooth*—i stop—i watch (use elms)—eye- / ale-
hued sun—fly aches: once he cuts chat, *lay over there*—
a layered theology / hump worship—slits dew
like blossoms—fold neat rune then gut—to drench
them bitter (rot)—see a drudge organ, a syrup
fermented, then a tang—a question cords
wrists / declarative hoof—emit *them*—you lube /
lush my tiny void—ewe tie: a lucid, iron hymn.

## [Shall I compare thee to a summer's day?]

my amateur she-hair, salt-scooped—elm
aura (theytremor / mental root)—develop me
(a shadow unfolding)—i stroke my gush, add herb /
ash / loam—*hello, thunderstorm*—a date: eat ass
(homo, honey)—oh sieves / teeth, i soften—eat me,
moths (flame / pond)—no odes cling—i did mix
softer / form nice rim—i dare even dimly a safe
butchering—curse arc in marsh mud (get no canyon
throb)—and lumen (my faultless theater)—
i spoon oils, frost raw hoof—he ate suns, set to
hunt hairless, horned shadow—neat salad / bright
linoleum (gone)—thornthirst: wine, sweet tea
nectar, honey—(*bang*) no more seas: see scale /
light's devolving—soft, i hole; *i* is a sheet / nest.

## [Devouring time blunt thou the Lion's paws,]

mounts point / blue shadowing—the rivulet:
waters thaw, nude and bored—hook hem over tree
(thigh etch / mutter-pocket / ear jewels)—if fern, seek
ebb, extend hand, hover—lurid loinlop—honing,
a rose sat / flaunts so (shames gold)—a neardyke
softwood fawn (lithe thread)—i omit wet duet—
a wall (set dead width / lewd foreshortening)—
i *he*—i brushfire—i bottomed (once)—*me* not *us*—
crow foam / ivory hush—envy low trot / rib's heat—
wintrier tooth whine—ensequin plant / hare den
or dune—too switch i haunted lilyman
cusp (taut fit)—gene rosary, boned, cement
(wet / whetted rot)—gild horny top / mossy deity—
i shrug a silvery moon—levy envy—level me.

## [A woman's face with Nature's own hand painted,]

wash a wound—faintest denim (a neon-raw patch)—
i smut amethyst / fire a sash—on smother spots:
a wet organ / taut bathmend, consequential
as ash in foam (fan of switching / weight)—less *shine*
than *gem*—brass her asshole (entirely tiring)—i fell on
cub, egg, throttle (wheeze)—joint hid gap in
hallucination shell—using horn i name
sadness: summon lacy snow—at haze themmule sees
waterfront, cries—to hunt foam—raw, dead
light got in—lushes a nettlehead, a truer wolf
den (ate foodheft)—beadmaiden deity
bending at hip—go tongue dirty hymn / spoon
cute, deer fur—*moon* (uses pearl): pinks hot, bewitches,
tilts, rusts—hear eventual deerboy, *hive, honey me.*

## [So is it not with me as with that Muse,]

white tooth musts its maw—i he-satin /
i she-beard—a pried oyster—vast but tiny
(red homo fan)—olives fatten—the hour sewn
to hand / hair / air—where fir / ivy, deer—ass heft /
me (moongroin, earpocket, a damp cupful)—
at hunt, dawn resins rain—scam he—sigh *them*, wood
-hard (waters billow / frill)—rare nights snap in frost /
his heat—hare thundering over—i haunt mess
/ blue (mute it, tower over it)—turn / yell—
a needle misbehaves—naively form it—
lush at tight throb—oh sing as hymn or code—
excessive handflood—air (a glad thinness)—
i eat theyhorns / wet loam layer—hemask fell:
opal wrist, rhinestone pelts, a tulip tool.

## [My glass shall not persuade me I am old,]

*pasture*: mold / moss inlay (gleam)—shelad
godhead—ate soft noon—*out* as a holy rune /
ebb—i hum—edenfruit stone—owls whither
into hay, doe, milk—dad-types exhaust hole,
froth, loathe, throttle a bud, cave at *they*—
hot mush tames me—finely bite artery
(men's wet throb)—lie: i shaved—hint: i hyacinth—
hitched tooth / antler—a burn, a new *he*—
holy eye of horse vertebrae—wolfsoft—
honeys it to low stir: blame fluffer—
*they*: crowache, periwinkle, thigh (hairs ably
burning lean)—offer: thread limbs—eraser
in morphine (honeymelt)—hunter as a witness—
even taking in a hue, i covet hag, bottom, stag.

## [As an unperfect actor on the stage,]

neon gutshatter—a forest can cape—
host's whip at side—i brushfire / hip sweat—
sweet crone urge to loom—the graphic i-me-he rift
(chews a stone)—house, hewn, stands breaking—new hart
forages frost roots (ate fury of it)—
river pelt ceremony sootheeffect—
removes stones (gentle moan decay)—twin hind,
hew branch / twigs—finger dot / men—i veloured homo
hole—ebb too meek—chest queenly (not
drag / pass)—fun gay tsks—men *babe* me (*pride* or
*cop parade*)—feed moon horns, vowel, folklore
(throat moth)—*he* / *them* / *her*: map red sexes to taunt organ /
alternative netherworld—howl it as oath /
hole—i trans so theysweet—wet vigil of *bone*.


## [Mine eye hath play'd the painter and hath stell'd]

heap name thinly (heart epithet held salt)—dandy
boy / butterfly mayhem—a fresh *no* at it—
*me*: shady hole—friends (myth), i tire / web—
repair / stitch a ripped attentiveness—
sunlit femur (hue / rot)—*ghost* like *phase, history,*
*mud, here*—lung (water to cure)—is deity if i rope
him (sash on thigh)—symbolic gown (slips in
width / swath)—idol's eyes' wet haze—hint: hagthin
androgynous—woven we do eye shoes / fat he-trees—
feathery meadow / ashen hind—enemy pantshiver—
say, *i hurt*—a gown worn home butters wet—shred *he*
to *hole*—anesthetize tip (edge) then grope
hyacinth / sanguine newt—tree rot—stag cry—tie
the house down (tent)—why *that* water (they break).

## [Let those who are in favour with their stars]

teahouse thirstoval—freshwater with iron
tip / a dual blood rush cups to bonfire—not
*house, room*—hips turn, fit, flush warm—witch
tooth / hoof—do i not ruin joy—*man* lurks
in *i* / i a refracted *vase* (further reversal)—to gape / piss,
taste me—blush at us, a honeyed grit—
i hit, mend, build—naive dress—eels rip there
and there (withering)—oil for toy / fray—
mouthful of tide / war hair—finger for sap—
i heft / cloud—i savor *son* refaced to a tin
hook, to queer orb—off, i harmonize *stud* (
felch / fisted)—gather into or hold—hart / owl /
phantom by the path—a doe / divan-level
moon—we boat home: rim every nerve red.

## [Lord of my love, to whom in vassalage]

volta: overwhelming solo day foams
starkly—mythtied orgy hymn / tit hunt—
wetting i eat het domes—hits bareness
(white monotony study)—two twists—
use history / a map (twitching wood / rose)—
am womanthrob witness, am eye—a wide stroking
echoed—i top / hinge to bottom—fuchsia-tone
thud / lily tang—a slow shout knots it—i hew bell—
i gag amethyst—lush winter mold (vast rot)—i've
spent water on my hair—i coast / cup fig soil—
porn plot / smut gap—a tender ladvanity—
fresh hysterectomy—how wet—too swept,
too thawed—*eden*: hoarse tomb—i toil heavy,
mothwoman heavy—me: horned-up to sweet, thirsty hell.

## [Weary with toil, I haste me to my bed,]

desire: i'm a they-boy / welt / thaw—omit
throb-eel (limp) / red star (fisted)—*a river*: to hew
/ hue (honeying bay)—adjust rib—net men—
does kink word-by-word—wet, sphinx memory /
high bath hem (woof)—doe ferns rare fur—my tit
so petaled i mouthe tanging—realize
i periwinkle, peony, pansy, edge—odd dome
(*do bite*)—dew's holiness and elk horn—choking
men as hag (might slay)—suit: vary it so
a host, empty stylish ghost, views—redsewn
shethigh (ink)—hung claw lay jeweling hit—
lube breakfast—doe haunch—i acknowledge stamen—
my manly thumbs (dying symbol / hid by it)—
men feed off liquid / thorn any forest.

## [How can I then return in happy plight]

chart: unhappy twining—lip *he* / hornet /
heft—tend bad biteharm—a frost tree
sings neonsad—it prays dew—they hipbone so
bad prophesying by daddy tint / tangy bush—
gem shrine / ashen god—i cut hair—teethe one
mouth harder—note: no scat—skin needs to
tear thinly—hot boot theme (*no police*)—
foothills afire—forearm froth / heftwilt—
tug my belt—*holed*: to pair that ethereal shit
to clutch at god—nimble hand sheen / raw ode shoved
into almond cipher, flower text, tight ass—
red light weight: star, shun, salt—knit nest / woven rope
(do tightly / rosy)—was bred dry—a moral wound
flinty, ringed—stags (torn) merge—the high knot gathers / mends.

## [When in disgrace with fortune and men's eyes,]

sweetened fang, runic ram, honeyed hiss—twin
witness: to pale tea, to blue lace—*may
i eat chub beef* (nods heavy)—trans odor, slime, welt,
fur—my lucky sodom (neon sand, pale fate)—
ripe omens: wool, chime, reek—oh *i* in night,
a needle kiss—if i fist them lush i'd work dim sphere—
imprints shade neat—damn stars—hag tonics—
joints tamely twisted to hew—can't hone
teeth / sing (homo yelps, thins)—styles gut (is famed)—
mistaken they lend that hyphenation—
a dirty, folk song—a lake: i (heart)break it—
gyrate: manflesh hangs—sheson (me): salt / vein / rut /
herd—severe butch bowl (terf hair)—messy gown melt—
heathen act / oystering—night swatch, mist knot.


## [When to the sessions of sweet silent thought]

oh unit—oh sweetest softness—night wets hole /
reconfigures man hips (smut map)—entomb
hymen oath—hag it—hoist a fig (suckling)—
*my need:* a window / lit maw—lewd hetero ass awaits
(he woofed unaware)—nylon cuntden—*sit
here*—plastic adds green diffusion—hind / horse's tit:
hard cave scene (gown slips)—one flawed cell, one
foam hymn—eat a thin god / an even-assed sphinx—
voice, tone, girth—see *evening,* a fragrance—
alternative wood / hole—*eye* from *owl*
or *a defacement*—both confused a moon
(bird, wasp, face)—not a wife, i honey hip—
i unbind leatherheft (hide network)—*i* if the
land or roll—order a dress, so a sweetness.

## [Thy bosom is endearèd with all hearts,]

thread trans hem (boys it)—a solid wheel—
abusive paychecks—hold whip—dig a den,
a veil—engrave *past*: snarl / thorn—gloved: lend oils,
widen, hold—(thigh thud) *hiss*—no rule (fabricate
one)—your shy shadow a moan—be a quilt,
a rune, a smoldering violet—i feel rot—oh my *she*
/ *her* do wet a hehand, a perfect wasp—is into
thin vein bleed (these do it tight harm)—nude
hive—reevaluate the riverbed—hot thud or glow
in gush—oh, the soft them preying low over
the dove gate—held raw rite—oh lisp motif /
housewife anathema—nylon titnod—
i tire—i dome—i heave—the swiveling
(all half, all tautly heathen) smoothed.


## [If thou survive my well-contented day,]

city shadow / neon flu—velvety rim duet—
to cum, hydrate—ravehowls shed thin—want butch shell
of *hunt*—rose / myrtle (burned)—ovary seance—
hooded doe, eelrust, ravenhop—city-self (seer)—
*me*: fat thigh epithet / new comet tit—more herb
to stop the deep nerve—bury hind by path—guy
rims me, mother of froth—horny velvet eyeerr /
hare hex (timid peg)—deep fetch—be honey,
cove mouth, hoof, hive—bushgush tang (let tint
sheets)—identify own warm grid (himgown, shag rug,
she-throb)—a blue horn, hag-shard, a rivet (hid), tit,
pocket in fog, hart, me—bear (a squinter)
bites bed as i top—deep hunt (recover / tend)—
effortless *they*—i root hair—i herd silver hills.

## [Full many a glorious morning have I seen,]

lush lunar fingernail—yes, move (*go*)—i moan
over a photo, eat mint, fennel, twigs—*they* is true—
i foraged sweetish hinge (old scent)—men gawk
(metaphysically sewn / gilt)—hehalved gem rain—
*us*: bitter root—needled masochist—pan
cliche—i stag, stone, haw, fur, lilac, key—
favored form: hiding—horned whistle / solar
slice—sweatier hunt (date is set)—nightgowns
rend noon—a resin: you miss me—held envy—
hip strap / rein—blunt wormwood—tall hymn
to cub hour / a blue shank—now mute, i eat—
oh, famished mouth, rim / tend—manchoker glow—
how mystified—hint: heavy horns—i tilt dome
(a hush, a swiftness)—no *them*-nerves—then a saintly wound.

## [Why didst thou promise such a beauteous day,]

hushed-up witch odes—you say, *i do masturbate*—
a tame hanky dot—warm cult / hive—to form *elk*
i name you backwards—let, yes, let me too
rhyme / verb—thyroid, tit, snot, keening hair—
to toughen, hurt (unteach it)—break tooth—hold gush—
*honeycomb*: a testament of rind / artery—
man cake / opal claw—noon flash fevers us,
ouch and ache—lathe turns (edged)—oh sew tit trans—
night myth: orgy poem / ash envy—sacrifice
the top's illusive thong—a lush theory: teeth,
welt, fur, a flower, the red side of brokenness—
fetches shaft gems, iron, root—rest / sob / chant,
*heart, heart, heart* (cavehush)—boyish slopes dwelt
in me—a cord, a sash, a rind all held tenderly.

## [No more be grieved at that which thou hast done:]

i hunt a thrive beam—teeth etch a god's wood horn—
rim ass (not ash) to unveil—devours hand / ferns—
son-shame instinct—*opal* as *bound cloud*—send
a deerskin blouse in two elms—dens that cave
unfilled—a manshine—a melt—vein task:
gush / twitch—prey theorizations: ram, asp,
crystal lung—peg / fist (moss in ivy)—harm
hymns hyacinth rings / sour seas—next, tie /
sufferblush tiny, ornate song (litanies)—
a dry cavity (hydrates to pet)—shave
unwomanly face (tag *femaleness*)—mild clap
case—a rich smut—vain howl—ivylined
den / synthetic cabarets—*us*: a seam
(freshwater motif)—oh, homobitch, rust sweetly.

## [Let me confess that we two must be twain,]

wet beau, wet cloth—maw / mitten (softness)—
love, undo us—hetero hairdo / diva lunge—
a hard bottom hilt (salt hit)—one meshes slow
the belly (boarboy hum)—tone: thin weep—
precious buttonhole—ewes sent to river,
to live perhaps—i laugh, i beast—*rune*, so
hoof / soft halt—i etch the cell over us—wig net
(deft hold)—got wet (smith silver oyster)—*a house let
go over time*: a meadow—entry: neck / heel—
a submouth—lash odes—delight me, wild eyelet,
burnt to ink—oh cure is *push down*—lone *him*
tooth hurt—hear me so thankful—meaty nouns
(touchstone) untied verbs (oilshoot)—
in the big meantime: history, porn, good use.

## [As a decrepit father takes delight]

lack titsag—i fed pet deer heartash /
shaved it hideously (dots of deceit)—echo,
dome, seam—pussy is to eat—tender leafrib
factory—theywarmth / throat dom / funk toll—
to hew worry, to hew fir—bluer he-habit—tart
hole (frat rose / *really oral*)—moon
in dishwater / pond / city set—told rent
time's here (void, knot, steal)—*gay*: term of
endearment / shape (mood / loin / sip)—torso
thuds—butch vest (withholding as switch)—oh eat ass /
stud (head)—cub chat (femininity): a fan
flatly grand—verbal play—oh i toy
with telekinesis (both hot, a bit wet)—*sash*
hyphens (them-hem)—heaviness, tip it, wait.


## [How can my Muse want subject to invent,]

unwets meat / scum notch—bent jaw (no ivy /
ore tooth, yet throb)—she hid testes up in warm vault—
gentle sex (unwelcome hetero taint / wont)
he to a pear grove (slurry pearfever):
*oh milk fat* / *gag fetish*—even they thin us
gant—i want to shed this glyph—a ray rusts—
i want to hutch a fresh womb root—*steed* not
*hoof*—*they* not *thigh*—(velvet lungdin)—i witness
bitter mouth home mint—oh, hunt, sweeten—trees
/ worms inch into heart—hyacinth sheen (loved /
held)—formational: the trans light—the bench
(blue-runed)—got alternatives to *melon*—
messy meshes—icy tea—i pulsed / hurt god—i foal us
/ rip *he* nets—sea ebb / inhale—put heat in the limb.

## [O how thy worth with manners may I sing,]

tiny moonwrist—warm honeywash / thigh
bath—let rope melt further—thaw a note
(water sign)—women with semen—cannibal (proof in
*man bites nip* / *dewruin*)—sow *he* thin—a ewe that
died—noises thrive (fluid, velvet
meaning)—lone doe (sore, ravenous)—old leaf
(sage)—amethyst orb (hip)—*i*: a nativity
hunt—teeth etch a silhouette (shadowed over)—
pant at overuse—cottonwoods web, lather, hum—
we veil / leash sweet tree ivy / stag rune (rue, too)—
feather out the hem, twist tight—tool on vein
to shave—he (cuddly switch) tooths tie—widen / gem *he*
into *womanhood*—hacksaw tune—teeth that eat
and eat berryshine / hip—chewing *him* or *home*.


## [Take all my loves, my love, yea take them all,]

*they*: my malt / loam—evoke a skeletal valley—
*he* / *man*: show that doubt house, that featherthorn—
holy, lethal ovum (lusty coven totem)—*larvae* to
*thin shells*—i water / bone—*desire*: fathom a mouth
or vermouth (ethyl of vice / vine)—seem to fly
over, to hum a theme of a consistently blue
body hue—styli tablet etch—effete mud vibes
(filthy tuft)—eyes flow / we beastflush / star /
fig / herb (get by he-flirt)—*eden*: too ivory—
*eve* all math / hurt / oat—to lush *eye* to glyph—
tang / edge foreskin raw—tie a silver toy
to joy (tweak horn, blow vein)—hunger (sans rant)—
low lilac shallows—we *us* or *hive* lacing slim
wet limbs (key to *i*)—plum stone, sweet fetish.

## [Those petty wrongs that liberty commits,]

to crypt—to mesh—shy, genital stem—brow / tit /
testament—momentary he-womb—i hear fish
(flat eye) fry subtly—hit / welt unabashedly—
if *oral mutt*, then *low woof*—leather strip (lots
of ornate teeth)—weed lung / hornet—abort
the beauteous root or fleshed area—tit abuse
(shadow want); a woman now owns no shame—
suave level: eel—livers ill with hard, holy pear
/ amethyst tea—tug that: *memory*—i free boy-sub
by untying (hydrates)—nudity / arch heat—today
i *her* (invite nether-hate / heel)—root dew
thawed—*butch*: word, fur, flare—took her to (rotate)
them to the bath (the ruby tinge)—eyes pry
at belt—a boytune: *yes*—bite fig / he / hymn.

## [That thou hast her, it is not all my grief,]

hart / heart (oh, light, soft simultaneity)—
hoarse, i've maidened badly—i dye tartly—
i lash shy, white thigh / affectionate hem—
shouttorn astronomy—all melee, i she-cave
(wild hunt orgy)—*vices*: luxe sense of life—
skeleton bowl caved, i suture too—oh, the hush over
us (even them, a smoky ode)—before *ass, hand*—
fern gravy—foam dome—she-knife rips fur, poetry,
me (a silent fossil)—yes, homo leg is ivy
(hand / hoof tends it)—neon ladyslur—farm thighs
(wholehearted *that's hot*)—i bond in cabin of
symbols (moons, handkerchiefs, art)—a toy
steed / boyfriend—a herotheme—an injury
heals—wet, blush of nettle, every stem a note.

## [When most I wink then do mine eyes best see,]

the omen wet, meek—*boyishness* tied / sewn in
(the nude edges / frothy scar, the plain, ivy welt)—
unhook epithet—silent, eyes held warm bone
like a bird—taking breath, drag dry dirt; drench
in woodhush / thawed herb ghost (*ash*: what smoke)—dot
of soft plum sorrow (who had, how, why)—shy, damp
earth—let myth coil yet arch, whirled, caught—
see, i gnaw the honeyed stones—shun his *yes*
(how we snub a boy)—deli dimes made eyeless—
gay veil / net—thin, bony *i*—oh, god in elk
herd, in peach heft—identity frames: wind, hag,
stag theology, hyphenated vessel—try houses: *his,*
*hers* (desolate seas)—i lithe it elegantly
(tightest hymndins)—we sand / herb / home (a gashed word).


## [If the dull substance of my flesh were thought,]

*hunt* to *cuff*—sweet, holy herb glut—*field* shames
*anatomy*—stud joy / witch lisp—i unsound sore /
feather its decibel—*the wood*: bog, fur, sun—*pop*
*art* or *theft*—omit memory—if souls shed water,
soothe them—hurt fondly (moan, tang)—dad tit
(earth's pure fatherhood)—fervent mom teeth
(*hand* forms *palm*)—*object*: hound hunting a table—
whether *we* holds *us*: able to speak in an echo—
tight mouth / gut omen—that salt habit (oh hulk)—
shortening plumage—the hole gone to waterfalls—
transhearted hug—thaw of bath—cut worm out,
eat it—humid ermine smut—only waists met
(overwhelming incense)—stole boy guts—
use *he*—*straight* ebbs away to doefever.

## [The other two, slight air and purging fire,]

*rot*: a wilder, toughening *ripe*—shaft girth
(reed)—white herb, web, hair (have to tie)—
the hurtsoothe, the rhyme—dirty fig stem
twisted, bent, split—sew he-moon's fattier shine
into fresh hem wreckage—eloquent, serene
dome of reset bone / heavenly tits—
no *me* (a blue, foam tide / wolf wife)—thin orgy
last week (cops show; only din)—manrod hits depth /
loud orifice (*men* to *sirens*)—i cubpelt /
shebust—*nests*: hedges, form, territory—few men
touch a seam (beard unwoven)—go back, sinew,
to your heat—flat mint echo—rift / hinge /
joint, too—a gelded blush—torn nightly
(hands / barks)—witching, i deadstag (organ / meat).


## [Mine eye and heart are at a mortal war,]

i'm a neon lyre, a ham tart, a raw deer—eat /
fist dewy cove—oh, sod, quit the hot night,
be my scrumptious tragedy—i weather / *he* thinly
(effeminate herhem theyriot)—dry moth gate /
lithium mesh—i throat to den—top had deathly
cairn—i ply wet lace  (severetched)—oyster's
bed (flattened)—that honeyed thud / pant /
peach paralysis—i shade tiny fern mania—
line is methodical (i'd pet / nest it)—
flaunts that grotesque heathen tooth—salt
rind etch—dyed, i emit red, trans vibe
(dynamic theater)—letter / rose / sphere—a day heat
hush—i woe us, nudest martyrs—i date a type
(the rant / rave gay)—throw dirt, oh, fields (a hymn).

## [Betwixt mine eye and heart a league is took,]

sex meadow / outbreath (keening)—a tail (eye it)—
what *stone anchor—hunt*: doe under dogtooth—
honey / dew / filthfoam—a noise (he marks it)—
tie thigh width—fever rose smooth—smallish horn
of empty—wetted, i *them*—hyacinth yourselves
(heathen pater / daddy—sequin tomb / tin tab)—
i tease her mouth—tiny garnets / eyes—*i'm me*:
hornet photo, hushriot, faghands—a vast deli
cooler (herby *um*)—thirsty eye pivot,
all flirt—testy wet sinew—a sea rhythm
/ moon hum—truth: hangover's tart scythe, that on-off
death whim (tidy sentiment)—i hew that hall
of empty sighs—i hit the preytune lyric
(metalwork / sea sashay)—that red edge in *they*.


## [How careful was I, when I took my way,]

hairy cake (wolfs, *yum*)—how a twin woe
birthed us—to cult a tree—fresh art turns
to mead (synthesis)—taut hum—guy-tit /
woman-fur stuff (shared hardness)—i flood torso
flowery—i thumb mouth jewels—*otter* as
trigonometry of swarthy fog—comfort wets me,
a shore / net—*sub*: an entry, code, deal, motif—
violet pervert / hefty hag—fat, furry eel—
evoke synthetic chant: i houndleap,
eat the feather, shout revolution—rough thaw—
*come, filthy sweethearts*—note rib, lung,
haunted heartspace—*rot*: wasteful mercy—map *moon*,
*tendon* beneath—this event: cauliflower,
froth, hives—daze or rope—fistripe hurtsavor.

## [Against that time (if ever that time come)]

*tit me*, that's the verification—game meat
(fed to eat)—hewn he-form / hilly scenes sewn
into shawls—*vasectomy*: hush that shut me,
cut seed short—add a cavity—tip bled salt,
stang—melt holiness, satyrhag—haunt the past—wait
a minute (sweet cherry and teeth)—styling *ache*
into *cove thaw / fresh hilt dew*—government
says, *invert self to hesonlad flag—dirt*
is a gender net (*i am a stone echo*)—*itch* met
*wish*—no torn, white denim—edge felt woken—
dry, hairy gasp—tense it—a flush (*damn, man*)—
leather toy hunt—grass fur to opal dawn:
*harvest me*—gather the wool / softest haunt loop—
nice cult—seahavoc slowing a lone eye.


## [How heavy do I journey on the way,]

honey the wound or hive joy away—
let's eat knives—why draw me anywhere
(death, a stone path)—coyote head tastes hart
head / femurs / firm half-heart (tender mysterious
reds)—*hit*: the way he waters—bite meat / tomb /
blunt root—sew delight dim—halt a peony
(bitchsoft) and winnow it—the sky ciders me—
i do peg him (flesh is reddened)—vertebrate moon /
month (spinal echo / knot)—our boy proved
thirst's tight, harmonious mess—eat then die—
clairvoyants hew ash raw—he, winehigh,
said, *right there—sun*: metamorphosis porn /
hope sham—muddy trans intro (that gin motif)—
hymn (join if bold): *my dears, we are dying.*

## [Thus can my love excuse the slow offence]

*she*: a cuff sweetly cloven—moon's cute hex
(*yellow bruise* / *fern me*)—depth foamed her—
*more water*, they hum—the howls said *hone* (fur etch /
rope definition)—*lust* or *nestling*—
lilywet butch / neon moss / raw hide—a pet fox
texts warm, new fowl: *meet in city bushes*
(thunderous hunt, openmouthed)—oh, wild nights
winking womanliness—din ode (the loop
in it)—soaped he-cheeks—path / wren ceremony
(offered feather gem)—sends *peel* or *bitter voice*
—sacredhush if lonely—garish fennel—i hill
velvety excuses (jumble of lush)—hoard a lot
of hormones—witching (see welt well)—fungi,
rot-mulling—generate shadow, dovetail, hive.

## [So am I as the rich whose blessèd key]

heed *her* symbolics—i soak ash sweet /
pornwet—merge silk / suture—caned hitachi-sob
/ -howl—river wove hunt lyric—hethey hues
neon plum red, stiffens, feathering out—lobo lip /
snarl foams at deer, foresees roseate horn
/ horniness—edge gone comically smitten—
hot holly tea—wild finch notes (ear perks yet
can't place air)—inject *he* / stone / raw
metaphysics (teeth, smoke, sea)—youth, its
wet head or hide (switchhood)—earth orb: herb,
moss, pistil, stamen—sleep (a nice teak / cobalt
unwinding)—hybrid of dim lispers / open
cussing—see weather robe woods—shy poses (veil
/ hip)—bedding glut, meat, hooch, point, break.

# [What is your substance, whereof are you made,]

awe-eye hebush furwoods—am tan oyster—auric,
a southerly moon glows thin, softens data din
or eye dishonesty (*heaven* an echo, veneer,
heady overabundance)—lusty noondew
-drenched bed (its fornication use)—eat
fatty doe / your ripe loam—i sit,
ache (no fleet / lube)—*skeleton*: a shy art,
a towering *i*, an unencrypted area inside—
i snap shot for a foot freak—he, spying need,
set the bow—oh house / round way of hot day—
oh hour oh boundary—pet ate tapestry
(even runes)—eye winked badly—ass whoop
arch—see a larynx / interval / poem—gut aloe
(a cool yearn)—i soften / keen—*noun*: to hunt, to bury.


# [O how much more doth beauty beauteous seem]

rub out a budache—sweetest homo, you home me—
herd the hart—*twig* woven into *butch* / amethyst
tide motif—blue fire works the area sore
with devotion—watercolor hit / hush—fetid
mold—feed pee—lay leash—tuck a shaven orb—
i'd hem, fern, hoof—eat, specters, utter us
uncanny (thorn at *son*)—hand slow as a glyph—
horse limb rest duet—sees chasm, swabs hidden murk—
fetish worn out irreversibly—oh hut it /
cud it—underdeveloped fawns / tea honey /
doom soot—thistle sewed nest so severe,
so weedtoothed—earth tires eastward (see fumes)—
you: a soft, uneven yodel (usual at boyhood)—
warmly thrust / slide tuft—i halve horn—he salts dye.

## [Not marble, nor the gilded monuments]

the gland bled omen tones—mint rum or
plum hooch—hiss (a wet, nervier spot)—lilyruffle /
bright behemoth—sheer sunset's clot—i annoy until
he thems—i blunt *son*, twist *her*—smut (sweatpainted,
wrathful)—lusts thaw, sweeten, unravel, soar
(raw flora stink / boot odor)—tumors (honey
liquid runs harsh from crow bowl)—sir earns snark—
*fig mold* or *ruin*—to rhyme *rye* cove,
blot, astonish—i eat a dull gem, an ivy din,
lush hell of city air—us: all fleshy pair—*ram* so *root* / *pond*—
thinly eye pole—arise, soft event,
water door—to swoon haunt the tight middle—
ride a fist—hunt me—joyless glottal he-rut—
i'd vine sinew unlovely, yield horsesalt.

## [Sweet love, renew thy force, be it not said]

welt sewn over stoic bone—feathery tide
ebbs the depth—*daughterly*: an opulent tie—
a tidy clay daub hides in *bog*—left (why)
to fern / night (oh weird prism)—marsh, moor,
holy hill—use of oval to eat / bough to thud—
yet why thin envy—ruthless elkwife's hunting yell
(soon a dwindle)—*gloam* or a knottier
flush—wild violet stops the pain—pleura / tree /
birthed colt (ink mane)—tie leash, see it
cinch—wet steed pant—hart or shrew—hew root, chew
(whiskey ache)—holy stone bath—met a netted
boy (herb omen)—see wet velvet form ritual
of winelight—i sect bluer—i hecalf / wrencall—
make a cursemess shimmer hermetic (owl, worm, or deer).

## [Being your ___, what should I do but tend]

boy served two lung hits—i'd tableau *hound*,
the nude hour to spoof us (many deer)—i *sir*
limper thuds—i aspen / eat toe—i volcano,
curl, love sore—deer roots *iniquity*
or *wild onion*, her herd outwitted—hued arch
forms thick waves—lyric: *touch hole, tying woe*
*to horn, bitten, broken*—fire uses ash scent
(*weed*: avid nounverb)—i cut you, honey—a hare's
snared in leather joy—i too quit / hum / show gut—
your boy perfume (fir / opera houses) as way
to gush / talk—shave a flank tidy (bound in seat)—
we arm / eye: a you-heap—hasty hookups (whoever
woofs too really)—unveils it—oh ritual
holy hunt—oh tidy knot, hinge us, a holing.


## [That god forbid, that made me first your ___,]

shrouded mother gods (amber fat, ivy fat)—a tilt—
iris (cough), oat (hunt), lupine (hurt)—*solo*: softer melody
of touch to churn cunt (oh red area) to a savory
verse—augur says *boyruin* / *bootlust*—inlay (doe
effigy or mature buck, bone / steel)—
imperfect boyhoods—rib, ulna, serenity
of punched tit—a mere ache—fence / banquet / acid ease—
juicy orgy union (i was ouch / tuft)—
*lechery*: ostentatious berry gush—i sorrow—
i glumly syrup—i mauve frothy—i eat eye, root,
body, hole (two)—hug it out to alloy / twin
myself—poor reconfigurations—folded
mothwing—labial hit—hot guise to awe—
i loam or bell, ritually prone—bluest ewe.

## [If there be nothing new, but that which is,]

bath (thigh intertwine)—hunt fib / sew echo
to ribs—*herb*: neon dahlia fugue—where bee, boar
or bear—lush, birching woman—i vain, i soften—
fresh chord (tunable)—doe confirmed
elk orchid—told a buck, *attach wood or raw*—
fevered she-fun (stunned cove)—oh i fur so
homo—baroque ink (sinewy maim)—go out; see
iris octet—the cairn named *dawn*—scans fir
thatch—lathes god wrist (elm)—he-wood duality—
do wet fist sorcery / moon-hue foam drop—
hew tree / tether—her honey, water, dew—bred them
sore—wove *herb* to *hermit*—lunate, he
fed them (was sir)—i roam you, forest /
shadow (grim evaporating)—bites, nerves, juices.

## [Like as the waves make towards the pebbled shore,]

bedeviled photo (water breaks)—am *he* (shakes / welts)—
harmonious thunder—to die, set stone
on chest (weight ache)—bicep hag—watching her foal /
drool—lewd taint—quaint fennel—*cords* so
*came*—talon in tiny vein—hot fig hit—
witch craw / wind warble—geyser hunt—too trim
(skin, hoof, leg)—ash sprig / dreg—toys elicit
wet motivation, handcuffing—hot and ghosted—
frothy mouthed flesh hunt—ass riot (ex into it)—
a bland nap—set silver bow—dye the laurels,
rust, and fruit—i seethe another forest—
bong / ditch water—shaft stuns—stony homo din—
daisymen—she spat in me—verdant holly set to
dry—hold wrist in, hesitant—gush (ripe peach).

## [Is it thy will thy image should keep open]

light (taut, sinewy, shy)—i milked hope pole—
showy, gay hive—i *they* tenderly—(*meat
thuds*)—broken tomb sublimely dressed—*house* or
*mimic* to hew *i*—sky's teeth / lake god, howl-shod
and hurt—seethe, oh tipsy thirst—tit motifs
/ doomsday spinoff—*memory* or *tether*—
*hi* or nudes—fundamentalists: *die homo*—
a *they* opens to a *he* softly conjured
(moss on grove)—hot toy hit (leg / haunch)—out
like smoke—whip, eye / vase (a tame entity)—
the furswathed moon, inveterate—let *my* dot
the patchwork—my leafy, oaten harvest—
sweet wife, without heart or shock—wheel sat, held—
flame, root, horn, file—water's foam / froth.

## [Sin of self-love possesseth all mine eye,]

assess soil—fetish of lemon peel evenly
turned—all ravens may play modally
in rood shades—terrify in mesh net
shirt—myriad neat woundings—i rode
their face, sang, came—*no kiss* is ominous
(touch stone, shatter)—focus on an hour—cup
fern (mood)—flinty horsewoman / dew fiend—
rims wool—lunar hunt: earth, salt, soil—
myth: *us* (bind, geld, sew)—mow shy femaleness—
panted (in width and depth)—quaint boy act—
eloquent, neon tower—lyric frame is avid
wolves of grief in lily quietness—
effortless, i map—i flit—amethyst heresy
(they-gay manifesto)—why a tying, a bud tip.

## [Against my love shall be as I am now,]

swishy son—am gate—am all bone vial
(jaw / cud / thorn)—i thud, semen, rind—oh i us (*i* narrows)—
*binds hard* (flourished on bed)—a lavish ow-whorl / hind
whir—silken dawn: women hunt silently or hush if
he gasps—that old thong, tear it evenly—
unleash bow with elkgrief—a sea-honed stone
(oh gravitation)—fed hiving horn—ass us
raw—sore hips gush yet—i antler (fine, *a stag*)
i fur, i hoof—craft me tiny woods
unfenced—a nice flagging—root us—i sank
home (furry man harvest)—clot the elm
sweet—lovely boy, guilty, hums *fever*—she-atom
likeness: heels, lashes, lean *bitch / babe* unity—
slant i vehemently hid length, hair, all needs.

## [When I have seen by Time's fell hand defaced]

fawned he-envy hefts needled, iambic leash—
diet: chew bread, sour fruit, hog (no cup / root)—
wet wood sews loose raiment—tide: frenzy hem
/ sea garland—nerveroom's all beast / tart /
heavy sanguine weather (hence honing,
hand (shaking), fog)—devote omen to earth—
swan warmth in doe foam—i *they* flintier
as i age—thin otherworldliness—stows / scorns it
(caveache)—fetish: unseen weight—hone trans
code, felted ode, fist sonata—*country*
*theme* as a huntmutt / a hurting—oh i rut
lacy, evoke tit dimly—thaw *male*; eat *woman*—
i chase its shadow (touches tang)—oh chant oh hit
oh fat wrist—wheat, spice, teeth—oh but a love.

## [Since brass, nor stone, nor earth, nor boundless sea,]

ensnared a clot—soon burntness or harnesses—i orb
—i oysterlush (a wet, strawberry tip, a mood)—
twilight blush—awe at horsehead halo play
(fantastic gore roses)—a hewn whorl notion
(one heart hull so warm / smoothed)—holy bush—
gay fist / fig—a bare, green walnut—thickets (does
kneel, sit)—oh garnet, bones, marrow—to *cusp*:
ends meeting so—*softly*: butter, sage, scar, too—
work at needle—a rim, a cuff, a toil—*he*
as jewel, dirt, melt, shift—mist echoes *embellish*
(*backstitching*: hand / horn / raw hold)—foot was soft,
praiseworthy. a cushion of blood—fib:
*he or she—man* veils me; in it a cloth sung,
halving it (sly, lean tomb)—i slink / thick my breath.


## [Tired with all these, for restful death I cry,]

furhilted fisters—*lyric*: oh hart, let dew eat
barb / reed / lobe—snagged throat so—
tendon and joint—they-idyll: rimming
a lush pond with neonpuff / star air—pry
hide (ulna god forms lilac hand)—*plum* eyed us
red—vale-mud mud—paints rune (tidy tree)—
wild plug cry—chaff / dirt—*gendre is not* [  ] *organe*
(gap is [*the tran*])—my swaddle / bind by sling—
nature gay (hound bayed at doe)—tit trim
(long roll / fold / ink)—*cynic*: saltkilled root—
triumphant lace—mystic lisp slid mild
dig at—cave, pond, plant—an *i* / tide (a cling to)—
*i was hote shitt*—blue ewegod fern ire—melt / hold
amethyst oval, a vein eel, a violet doe.

## [Ah, wherefore with infection should he live,]

hewn *i* (oh in watercolor)—i flush / feed the hive—
switchy hag canes me—it ripened ripe
(sheaves bound and thigh)—*i* (a lit cave, a myth)—
hyacinth (sweet fossil) i laced it
tight—i hand / latch / spike—i see housefly in maw—
i leaf / sun—i envisaged god, thin, leashed—
lurid, horse boy—dewy eel—a hot, sticky pun—
hair, tissues, roses—she-wood (conifers,
herbs)—oh, periwinkle wound, shut any vault—
bush (god) by river (god)—lushlove of *both* (all tinge
/ sore)—*oh, queer fawn, botch his hexhunt*—
a pond oversimplifying a sun—*hound* as
*a howlmess*—hot hot hot—weathered swish / ash—
see a body lit (force / salt / shine)—*bend* as *song.*


## [Thus is his cheek the map of days outworn,]

*coyote*: a raw shift / hunted pose—*him*s husk /
evenly dew or snow a field—bone us—add a width,
forbear it—barbed fern of wetness—rig *oh* as
*throb*—i bud or wring natal vision
(foreshortened god head)—felt bees set
the lyre—the hush gnaws so—we are fir / crop
line left on an ass (echoed)—i cove odd
and eager—they, blue as a deer, fade yet come
in (leather, honey, hum)—questions arise: oh
tell how to administer fun—lunate art
summons moon / girth / fang—keener ear
hears bugdrone intensity—bow bloods
tip—trans foam, trans dome—hoard a hue
(of water, of beautyslosh)—raw, sweaty oath.

## [Those parts of thee that the world's eye doth view]

soft shadow tether—she loved thaw theory (petite
mort tang)—handhewn fountain—the thatch gets hot—
hull gouge / hole satisfaction—the outed eve—vest,
no shirt (trans combo)—see a fur event / gem duet—
write, *trusthurtthud*—a caw, a window—prissy hood /
attentive seam—oh sweet, stout he-bough—oh tensing
drench—soapstone hounds (artifice / tonic)—
her breath honeying—when they eat shafts
they omit tooth (thankful boy)—needy, i
bead testamentary seeds—*hunt*: shy, guyed *hi*—
lush hutch thrust—light (hair / horn)—we see, the eye got kinder
drawn away—threefold tethers fold me—*folk* is
*they who myth how*—stud to that horny cub,
*hit me* (growls, *that's hot*)—touch moss (devotion).


## [That thou art blamed shall not be thy defect,]

held (rhythm) to *be* held—taste a cobalt tuft, an
arm / err—salt knifes the wavy sea—for *red*:
*their meaty button*—aspen focuses
friction (waver / heat)—set leash eats sinew /
blood (generous broth, devout sap)—top had
big *with* energy to froth me—earth ode (two):
velvet and wood—corset (bitter husk)—he, *feces*;
me, *no shit*—i rune / pendant—spat pear / sutured
body to bush (day gush)—hump toy / fasten a sash
(incontrovertible gash)—deer had orgiastic
shine (rainbath ecstasy, pyre it)—they stoop
to pee in revelry—enter, mauve god,
sit (confesses hookups, filth my maw told)—
homo hush (too outlandish)—new stalk greened soft.

## [No longer mourn for me when I am dead]

hew fern lineage—moon mound—ram rod—
they herbyell, all strenuous *he*null—a lash
/ light drawn into wild grove—a me—a theft—
mothriver's mothsilvered wowfolds—twillwilt
habit—i rose myrtle / neonfemur (an i-dye)—
oh violet node—oh fist (a tryhurtwait)—
house aloft in the woods—*i*: buttery gutgrowth—
*i*: makeshift doe / he-eulogy now on mink hunt—
*you*: hive / silkiness—*you*: a rooftop
with no leap—cup / swan me, my hard hip code—
*a chrysanthemum* so *a reopened room* so
*clove bewilderment*—i tuft you heavy—lye
(lush, ash dome)—i silk, wood, wool, rot utterly neon—
oh i mummify (a neck, a wet, ornate god).

## [O lest the world should task you to recite,]

oh, elk lord, root out—sweet chastity led us
into their mouth—metal hull, odd wavy sieve—
former hermit (dog at feet)—levy adequate
hit—grow a riven peony—cry of moonhunt
(viewer unveiled)—you loom loss—i stud / use *us*
as tether—wonderment, i fem / moondoor—
noon praises a deep drudge, a machine
purr—godly hind nightlilt—twig / arm, a walnut
tree (shameless teem)—sun out of a lily (ivory,
voluptuous)—*feathery*: feel no metalwork
disharmony—we dim ruby eye—ebb me—
devour hormone astronomy—*omen*: a line—
barbs thigh (thorn immediacy)—oh, tar whiff—
oh, long, naughty noon—riotvolts—doeswish / thud.

## [That time of year thou mayst in me behold,]

amethyst heft—blue moan—i doom it earthy—
a worn elegy, a fresh eel—neon nod / vowhowl—
soothe glowing ass / dank he-sheath—i pouch *butch*
bent into *beard*—sew charred surrealist sigh—we *he*
to hide (smutty he-itch / woeful stagshine)—
sweet taffeta trash (i'd stun)—*sheen*:
bodylight—thick thwack—a handy (babe: *yawn*)—
distasteful catastrophes—an endless hell
of cis things—heel to mouth—we use fringe
to house heat—hot fields, hot hay (hints
at *bush*)—doe eats withered mint—*he*, per ex,
*ate shit* (munch on, bitch)—why is *wad* wit—shroud
(chastely tie) to rot / gem / porn—he whisks vermouth, chives—
velvets out the hollow—melon hit / hug—waterlace.


## [But be contented when that fell arrest]

sweet blotch / burnt earth—flatten need—
a boy, all *wham* / salt lily—auric wreath—
*i* or *fleshiness* (intimate myth)—the line
reaches—*hilt* thaws to *warm hole*—i'll hit (flimsy
width, no hurt)—their soviet hues—sweet woe
open everywhere—start the staccato
thud—i ache—butch hair / hart heaviness—wet, he
fits—bitten, he pits—*ripe* met *rot* (a rhyme)—
night, house, rosebush (felt hottest at fold)—
feather (body)—gem (body)—modern, wispy
queer (wet, cotton hankies)—chaff crowds
the fear—rose bee bee dome—bottom
whines (thin witchcraft)—tit has tooth oath
twist—hand sheathes tit—maidenhair thins.

## [So are you to my thoughts as food to life,]

oh to oyster out a soft holy *i*—a smudge of
gore—water sheds a season / snow / tree (shut door)—
sad nude of *hoof*—i cut rope—felch hysteria—
*ass* is *faith* / *existential downward hum*—
*no*: round, jade—a pansy *no*—neonraw,
i scent—i gush larger with bluest delight—*i*, no, a *leaf*,
*stone, bone, walnut*—i thin to *guy*—cooweb /
warm, butter heart—semen dots the pelt—dye *he*, lay
it out—minimal flash of yellowness / tight urge—
trans daddy can bone boy—lake-flavor
rippling—sings *rune* to gods / houses—
the woods hum us a soft, batik room, a very
dainty bud—diet: pussyhoney (afraid
to oralanal, to lingual wrongly).


## [Why is my verse so barren of new pride?]

i envy she-domes—brew fern, sip yarrow—
aroma of fat cooking—quivers ran rich
when they edged—*i*: a silt motion, a witch—
sound-endowed mound—notch tang—*maps* to *forest*
(wholeness)—i eat lily helmet / raw rivet—
deep, tannin devotion—wake in need
(*melt my wood*)—salt, lavender, rot—they-math:
hyphenating hide—witch throws eroded deer rib,
unveils it—works a wet woof, a wooly eye,
a nude moon (vulgar, red)—meanly a sly tit
swells—distressingly rawboned moods
aplenty—washing pagan dead—nest / iris /
loud fold (sewn tiny as a hind's ear)—
mold hollows stag, silently it veils it.

## [Thy glass will show thee how thy beauties wear,]

eulogy: this saltwater washes the hebowl—why i
ache—*push me down*—*thirsty* is *wet*—i lay out
my thin pelt (lavish bewilderments, vacant air)—
the stud flogs (sonority, heat)—moans knit a habit,
well raw yells—thick wrist, slow hunt—high, shy
hum (edge, fist, hover)—yellow rim, ovate gem
(bay it natal)—shy dye tsks swath—hot, holy mud—
moist hetero teeth sing tipsy rivers,
act on loamy arc, think, *why not men, too*—
match not that womanliness—sub takes dildo heft,
holds it—horn / fir (recurved)—hybrid's need / lament:
am *they*, not a twin / fake / con—aquatic end
(she coils, thaws)—of eel: took out of fist—
hop-hum chant: *oh boyhalf trickled in trees.*


## [So oft have I invoked thee for my Muse,]

evoke hum of aster mood—vein is hefty
/ curvy—in sauna steam i fed finch sand, roses,
ivy—honeys a peel—magenta she-rut
in the pines—red-hued oyster sap / deer
thigh—he-tit gaiety—boned omens—that gush hunt—
a frothy, lacy glove—a fat din—neon (
held / harvested in dew on a stag)—feathered,
gaymaned god—eel vibes cunt ajar—
pelt / hide (mythic cub motif)—how sore—a top
bewitched in sheen of antifurl—one hones
into wettest rhythm—oh dour buds / skeletons,
sway, draw a tight hedge—breastcrescent
bra notch (lunar daddy tat)—salt / mauve
to a gruesome hardening (any hairs cling).

## [Whilst I alone did call upon thy aid,]

dahlia slouchtilt / a wild peony din—
let my lacy song lavender—a he-heart / leg
/ bay—sour bud ceremony—i cream stud, gnaw
their nude stick—develop gay man's *macho*
(loverly swag)—mouth a gent nervy (eel / tit)—
a pervert, i'd eat flowers—heaviest horn
(fatten it)—to hyphen they wove the dot,
feathered it into boyshape—sang a he
-duet (hated it)—rosethorn welt—even ash held
the rhyme—*i:* votive body—be a hot hag, fur
and fat—honeythick ache—*undid* of fern
tip—love is a wet hone / throat hunt (heed bite)—
hoard that thin moonheft—hit hewn sky hatch
(hefty thud)—oh woes (a hypothetical sweetness).


## [O how I faint when I of you do write,]

i yawn—i wife—i houndfroth, too—*woe*
is a tin house knotting me raw—redo puberty—
nips frighten so (*thistle seed*)—palm a hind / hare
(softdome fugue)—enema tip reek—too gay: a mink
waistcoat (obscene)—your hide / sinew hurt (
deleted: plush hart at rut / he-sis, homobabe)—
i char rosy rib meat so—if *fur, yank*—
*morphed:* pour oily boy / faun—an altar (wild
wheat, plump, all to lay)—wool held flourishes
then (spun otherworldly puss-hue)—*doe* is diode /
a door between—bitch, i work glass arm
orgydeep—fold / fluid into bald lionhag—
he-shaft bead—a tinier cavity hewn
with love—say *craw, dewy moss, amethyst.*

## [Or I shall live your epitaph to make,]

i tie hour oath / milky poplar leaves—
view true river, honey, hut—i trans a moon (
*oh, moontran, rhyme me, eat cunt or cake, defy*
*thin fable, gather wool)*—theme: apricot (lung
-soft oval hull)—manic he-mare harmony / fir melee
(modulate, oil the notched song)—*hug it lower,*
*tang me* (rivulet anatomy)—echochambered
into dullness, a heel—men eye my wishbone—
bluegreen *yesmommy* love—antler hunts
(red etch / nectar)—i yellow so easy—he-dearth
sad-ebb—i eye lunar teeth (our long horns)—sage
feathered into the shawl—horse bled raw lard /
unlovely lump—ivy (the lush theatrical hiss)—
hew the bottom / ash—bare thorn / femur—men see the veins.

## [I grant thou wert not married to my Muse]

i am wetting my hurt star—rude omen: *root*
*root root* (interlinked as *myth*)—awe of taut heat
hewed with wrist—odd citrus aches—deer
break glossy in the fire, furcove it—be job's
dank, funereal *he*—i swoon—i tart—i gush a
modern nymph (filth / pity)—await stag, iris,
water sheen—*area often tender*—doefrock
(*mist*, the softest hem)—forestpanged rib, arm, eye
(velvety haven)—oh oh to add wideeyèdness,
drenched in color / sweat—*i*: a chestnut hart,
ritualized flesh, taut myth—try wry pour
then lip bitterly—dawn is greenly round fruit—
*tug bits tighter*—neon's brighter need is a damp
blue—witch seeks bee or doe, hidden in the sea.

## [I never saw that you did painting need,]

*red*: pain, twinge, honeytaste—i vain / dud
*hetero* (painted forgery: *fountain* or *satin*
*echo*)—dug out, i undo it—oh index of dyed fur
and tart need—to top freer, *he* ebbs /
i thread ornate she-rune—levy rope for tip
(to mouthe it sly)—i brew exultant, fleshy hag gown—
marrow etch (hoof, moon, hill)—*quoted*: sad rot
of words, atrophywork—oh i go wet hunting thaw—
in lush ceremony i mud, i piss (fetid toy)—
lilygod hymn barbs me—elm bough switch—
gin perfume / tin aura—i tie boytomb
in bow—rib nerve got delightful shadowname—
my serene eye: a horseloin rite—if off, i velour
robe—tart pussy—divine heat (soon in peach).


## [Who is it that says most, which can say more]

man shows waist / rhythmic sashay—to ice, to
out—oh i ruin so salty—eat hare, pear, hyacinth—
i cut hem shorter (moon)—fine side sinew—
lush, queer hour—coax lily / peg hard—we hew / mew—
lewdly intertwined—help on a hunt (path
through nettle blossoms, lacy moss)—tend a jilt
habitually with scruff—one to teethe
hysteria thin—i go / use door—*you satisfy*
*without subtlety*—i womanhip—i cry
nectar / warm metal—saw doe unhooking aster—
saw euphoria cuntfisted—*chants all harm*
*away*—vein rhymes *tree*—rim silkhedged
beau—lose our boyed statuses—*runic*: so gaudy
and awake—oh i cup fire, grip ribs—snow sores / honeys me.

## [My tongue-tied Muse in manners holds her still,]

hornless, i yell at men—i redden tit, summon gush—
to mimic leaf i open (rich swell)—*hurry, copy domes*
*here*—hit / tend raw circle—hollerstag quiver
(biceps)—*i*: a rude oral shape / fleshly smutden—
work wood loose—it drew us, this god thorn / tight thigh—
turn manly, little, elk neck—deer arc slid
into the moss / drapery—verify that flab,
flower, nipple is fondled firm—no *he*
destroying you—piss hiss tea rite—i aura
on the sheets (too damp)—i trans form, a demigod
(oh boyish waves)—out to tune mouth tightly
(no wolf chord)—undried basket / herhomo thighs (moss
repeats, fresh froth)—hot herb odor, wet scent
funkscything room—beat, thump, feed me figs.


## [Was it the proud full sail of his great verse,]

pelvises hold soil / tart fruits—a ewe / fur hag
(hoof oozed fire)—*our*: out, open, public—*sly art*
as *mighty orb*—*hunt*: see a hind dart in—i tip / rhyme
the winemaw, grow to be her-ember—knit my thigh
(oh tapestry)—i waist, rib, wrist—i gut, hips, tits—
damp earth / hard violet sect—a tuck—a tomb—
herpes hymn—oh, noon, ignite—birch trees'
eyevoids singing—mad, i harvest him—
i, a gem, thorn , hail, ash—bra off, let fat
uncinch (my high, white hill)—sling wit / let leg
cross—boysalt: a motif / accent (on veins
a confection)—wash oyster knife—farm /
noun the ancient eyelid—blush, ruin, wolf, cup—
embattled enamel he-tit—a thick fern end.

## [Farewell, thou art too dear for my possessing,]

forage for seed—torso (pale swath, mostly ruin,
tusk, and smoke)—how tiny a he—nettletough, i
sting her—froth (cavewater, horsethigh)—let eye
tie tan hare—to be maidenly—elms rend
the hunt—brotherly dogwood, thin bay, fig—
*sinew* is cord—high fem theyraven—red star
stiffening—i tug moist chant—seawife hair
snags—meadow caving—sip tinny bark tea—
why thorn soft stone vowel—why enknot gay / tight hunt—
moongate theist (use smoke, light, raw vomit,
opium)—stag orgy—worship ring (softening it,
tonguing)—ate bog jam—omen: smeared mink—etch
death hat (helm)—avoid deer fat—harsh statue,
its utopian knuckle—gnaw seam—brighten.


## [When thou shalt be disposed to set me light,]

oh plush welts / obsidian edge—test (hot them
had mites once)—pearl ceremony—nifty
flip—unsightly half-god eye—*i* mans, tits,
turns over—oh woofed-at—oh purgative rush—*not-hurt*:
to sweeten (wine, skin, maw)—*aching banquet* is *bed*
or *nude top* (spy toy, want)—*a thin scar*:
draws a comet, a faint line on the field, a cut
on her thigh—coltish mustglut—inlay (woman
bathing in woods)—i eat air / belly
fat—horn / glen levity (the blushingmoon god)—
jade in holefroth—my tit tissue
(vague *not* / lobe)—*give head*: tend magenta,
hothouse blossom—i levy genetic
throb's raw length—a myth: fog, water, lilyfrill.

## [Say that thou didst forsake me for some fault,]

stark *sad* of doe—fruit tautly foams the hem so—
wolf pelt / moon mane—induce chant fit /
mild fetishes (salt, metal, silk, horn)—pagan yaw
of neon sea hag drinking a steamy scent—
icons unfold: horse, stag, hill—*to mate* / *calve*:
torn to cup, edge, harness—i foamed
ring glassy—the willow, slim-knifed, lacy—
swanlike goregarland—quaint linen—a colt acts
drunk—fleeting boyness (by that am woman /
new marsh moon)—tat bled (held yellow sleeve)—
tight condom (free)—i do owl us / opal thorn us
(floral hunt)—add opaquely ancient coal—
straight fondles violet—be *way* female—
oh, harvest moon, i mouthed fist, tumor, wheel.


## [Then hate me when thou wilt if ever, now]

runewoven omen halfwhite with teeth (
snowblown herd, red ewe hood, stylistic stem
[note skew])—pit of mouth / jawbone—i themfire
forest—adorn / fold *pain*; don as torn
coat—*womanhood*: she / thorn / wreath—the ships dry
careworn, moored—quiet cow head, a fern—
i grit / nova—winter hymning a doorway—
dig out hornroot, eat pulp, or swerve
(distill to malevolent tea)—he wove a fume
ring—hipheat pewter—fetish theory / doe events—
test he-limbs—touch satin, aloe, stone—
soft trans of toy's girth—we river / tuft hem
with frothiness—we oceanmaw—wooden horse
disc—sweet he-rose wisp—oh, moon, mottle, fall.

## [Some glory in their birth, some in their skill,]

i riot sleek—loins met (rhythm)—girlish, i boner
(berried stem)—i wet shoe—i fetish—*icon* or *manhole*—
enamel thorn / fig—hunting game, hilt slows deer—
i'd shear use (no homos harmed)—*twink* (his rhinestone
nova / rune-eyed amulet, jar, cup, dish)—harthush
shaft—be *i*, intense river thaw / doejoy—
eat meat, use it—sour, trans peach, mulberry
-tart—length (bone, tree, line)—be sea / isle
both—brotherly them-hag—nest it, hive it—
warmhearted cuntness—hare plight or chant rot—
gowned elk, fat boar, shortish horse—*hem*
as lavish beefing—melt hope and adorn it
with hound teeth, chalktaste—anatomy's rite
(maw, claw, dome)—i knead her (salt, amethyst).


## [But do thy worst to steal thyself away,]

salt oyster bowl—wet shaft—*duty*: to hay
/ foam the field—trans fur smut—i roe / ore,
let vanity rot—holy hill / glade—neon fawns
tuft, hoop—pond veil / feather din—stone
(soft, tender weight)—now a foresthorn tone—
feed him hewn, amethyst filth—oh lean net,
beg, tease me, eat brittleness, too—
hump hand (we hunt hot hydra)—hot itch (noted)—
cinch *woman* thin—nudest texts—to nova: mint,
holly, thorn—synthetic foamdelve (tie it
at hip width)—idol: a fat peony,
a heavy poppy—hit holy, ovate depth—
soft halfbeast—stern lush woods (ate rabbit
boy, tasted honey)—mount *want* like a fist.

## [So shall I live, supposing thou art true,]

*i* (lush pulp, sea light, tin vase, sour root)—
*seed* as *bonefluid*—slack he-cave (video
streamed)—smooth, unlovely heel / metal twig—
coo the oath rhythm—stealthy periwinkle
fever—thin ochre need—none ate (hilarity)—
thicken *thorn* to *fang*—wither / honey at cane
lash hit—soft, hairy root—yank less (semen
stain)—kind: rinds worn melon, ferns waist, rawdogs—
butch tried head (aced it)—neon rye vein
flowers lewdly to velvet hue—aesthetic hand
twist (they gush)—hag to her *he*—thorny breastwork
stitched (yellow ghost / nettle lesson)—bone / husk hunt—
booty welt / dewy thigh—elksuave hare pop—
synthesis: wive roothurt / wet theyfawn).

## [They that have power to hurt, and will do none,]

heathunt / yowltend—thaw over horn at doe lip
(that's honesty)—dot dot: *dew*—hot, moon thigh—
homo hems hover even glossier—states want:
*to consent*—wood, mold, pelt—mud in a vat—
hyacinth hedges—they rig torn veil—ears'
bend / arc—hand at hip, femur (nexus soreness)—
deer horn, horse dress, taffeta (claw it, honey)—
sexsour, cell ache / bittersweet, den froth—
rim (mouthes moss)—fresh weltsmut—ewe / tree
(shade unity)—i let night flood violet—
whine if wet—eat clit / soft ember (bit of a hunt:
tongue's width / heat)—breeds ass—ivy bite—
*there* (rubs one out)—wets, *try fist*—grinds the seeds—
fem sews red floral, leathers waist steelthin.

## [How sweet and lovely dost thou make the shame]

stone, loam, steed, smoke—theyoval thud—hew / haw /
gnaw at nail—fern this herhair—cock reek
hot boy (taunt bud, edge)—a fetish: pond myth,
hound's eye, titstitch—hone swoon (asswelts)—
they ghosted (that fatty tonal result)—shy to
piss—mythic moss ring—one oval tuck—*to man*:
to disunion—panties' fabric (a pinker sad)—
neon limbrhyme—all sass / penetrating
octave—sow thigh heaviness, oat, moan
(oh hoochbitter / ouchsweet)—if thin, eat hair /
boot's lovely curve—*herb* (the weed variety)—
tense, tin laugh—fantasy: leather, cord, satin—
dig edge (half liver / heart)—tie hare—pokes tear
(delight is odd silhouettes)—knead flesh here.

## [Some say thy fault is youth, some wantonness,]

homo anatomy (say *testes*)—wet, noisy sunflush—
stagdress manthigh—easy peony—cutely root
for comfort—harvest a lean lad's bulge—send a doe
home—touch / gather salt—tsktease to frustrate—
heathen god of neon queens—fir, tar,
swell—she webs—little, male bee (dew, jet
[the stone], resin)—rest hoarse, hetero area;
melt into transness after—thud drug—thread dot
(sly themmoth feathers)—my mawbowl bi-tang—
foal's brushlike head—somatic knell—i alto
to hag womanly—hazy tits, raw edges, a hum—
lush tufts' soft taste—gut hill / earth—dew to honey
the bush—stoic toe riot (novel sound)—
tight hoop is *rays* or *genuine embodiment*.

[48]

## [How like a Winter hath my absence been]

enhymn / enleash—work a bite—a bee witch
ties elmheft lathe—featherer of peony urge—
feastfevered, i tat shank—a dry, wheezing shawl—
trans vers(e) creams—he-deer bowel hewed by
warmth—stem vein, made mysterious, tides me—
i cinch, hinge, masturbate—unwire tit / he-gem—
tend he-fig / rub pewter moon—i nab anther
(red as slim head / elk dew)—of two: corset rib / wide
boyishness—nude tedium—meattaste
of burnt fat—drape hand / furs on hip—out *he*
as radiant powermouthful—messier sheen
at wrist—devoured any harm / he-beauty—
refuser (chastity, withholding)—lie so
i petal wet (ask to)—hind's old antler, hag ear veneer.


## [From you have I been absent in the spring,]

sing beauty (nerve, bone, hip)—*man* or fetish
(pared resin hilt)—mild pulp / rind—hair dews so—
*history*: thin, figurative hyphen—tap out
(it hurt)—untwist glyph—am a halved head, a hand,
or bowl—see the transitory *them* fly (endless
failure of others)—find rune (doe); now find
doe (rune melts)—my clumsy altar smoke,
rhyme for *wreath*—deplore plumpucker / wet rot—high
-wild hair / wettest din (oiled, horny,
ripe)—i open ram's red horn (teethes on veil)—i
gutter (wedge *wife* here but tie softly)—*bush*:
a floral fount, a rowdy eye—prostate hunt
(wide want, meaty yield)—i lust an oyster—
i shade (shadowshadow)—i truly pity white.

## [The forward violet thus did I chide:]

shift water, divide color—hidethud,
heftthud, holetwitch, thaw—let stems salt—*steed*: eye, sinews
teeth, rump—ferns ripple—boy had violet form—
complex fetish (wolf, honey, cloth)—wicked horns
(stony hair)—moss is honesty, devoutly gloved,
inched in—any old threefold myth—
homohard hard—my lassfat, rib, and jut—no
froth—salt ruins the dress—a fly, odd, neon
as *omen*—oh hind heat, pear bulge, wrist shine—
hid raw root throb in forest—*hold* and then
*hand* and then *thirst*—boybody bra (a hexer)—
now relish pit fur, thigh fat, soft hole—bird
nova (plumage heat)—fed a rune thicket—
ceremony (i note utensils)—doeflower ode /
stud's bloomruin—tore lore to chew the fat.


## [Where art thou, Muse, that thou forget'st so long]

glutton eats the marrow—to huge, to hush (softer,
ghostlike)—thaw thigh hotly—*camp*: festive heat
or wondrous seethe—oh nymphs (sly tufts) / tongs
(brass, length to pluck)—night reined joy, bedsweat,
the deer—gut me (transfigural sternum)—red of
embers tempts neon lust—in yielding
i tend—amethyst teeth sheath—*astrology*:
a moving glyph—tans deerskin (blunt death)—
eyes fur / velvety mess—sorcery is smut / a ewe
hewn (reverent meat)—hair (ivy), ankle (fig)—
a fist, a bee, a cry, no, a deity
(needlework hysteria)—piss vase—dimmed seep
of taffeta—rim me velvet—hag sees my waistline
(hid pecs / dry cove)—*hankies*: to knot the soft runes.

[O truant Muse, what shall be thy amends]

turn small, amethyst hand—we toe a bush
(freeday nudity / theycunt gobletfroth)—
*tend* (*body* haunts *botany*)—devour hem / pelt—
hounds eat hindgod in forest—i too tide,
warm, womanlike—yeast, honey, salt shut up
in flowersex, its odor—oh i round / cult / hutch
rabbitly—eye phony lunate cutout—sat
in dirt—fist extreme sub—bent vibes—
cub bush (nude, asleep)—the water bodies—i omen
/ echo—soon i sit—textures (fleece, linens,
mud, velum)—godlike i meat at *bitch*, *homo*,
*fag*—i set a taboo (deep bend)—oyster
wood soft—i *he* the me (he-tunic chafe)—they
-hole hem—*swan* meet *swag*—he shone moonsick.


[My love is strengthen'd, though more weak in seeming;]

emit he-lung hiss—verse / dogkeening—men thaw my root—
oppressive hellhush (stone, wool)—stagheat
(thigh / mineral dome)—he swerves then cites zodiac—
to hue, whip sweetly—rough horn, bent, severed,
burnt—shadow weaving opulent net shrine—
i twin *tit* / *watermelon*—who's gayest (why)—
*mold* so *mourn*—night fleshiness (armpit,
a ripeness)—hip forward, drops tight peony
(showiness)—unearth salt stem—let man top
this time (hung)—herdhush hymn—unhand nth flower
bud—*them*, vibrating, wet—oh sultry chubuse—
hand / wrist (modeled)—nosh on sweet egg-rot miracle—
method: firm mouth / elk shrine—eerie elegy, too
(cow duet)—oh you boys, all nudism / wine / glut.

## [Alack what poverty my Muse brings forth,]

raw thorn glyph—i say, *fuck me*—starvetomb /
thin paper ash—oh he dug witch, too (scarves,
for showier theater / long blur)—am tame
(he binds me)—wide tapestry had a hind / heat
of briar, neon, mint—eel item maw coo
(slick play)—arouse a pagan note—oh red fears
(vein, meat, guts)—violet (horny bonnet)—quit
discouraging me and geld slimly, end in
wonderful tightness—omit tin, reinvent
womb—test that herb—flower ejaculates
(vers top softens)—honeyed arms rot—
furs turn to organdy, filthy lace, too—sage,
mace, chrysanthemums—divine moon ranter
soothsaying—we unlink—you show your wools.


## [To me, fair friend, you never can be old,]

foam endured—veil cronebone, fray it—
sew iffy hetero ruin / eyesore—dye *you* raw—
systematic hurt (shoewelt bruise)—cruelly nosed
fur—a hot mesh dress (overt peek)—horseform theism
(manebeauty in stone)—throw out urge—slurped lust,
feverish in openness—choose: eat ass
or serpent—i jeer / spur / fable him (hunter hunted)—
*we*: sheer—*we*: soft ruin—satisfying, i cherryache—
that unladylike body / heat—hide a.a.
from old friends—given cue is *eat peach, pear,*
*yellowest wheat*—sir's thick moon shines (thud, thud)—
honeyed cavity / maiden dome—bite he-name,
hew it—oh feather—oh fragrance—oh fur—i'd sub,
obey stud—summon weary ewe, rub deer's ear.

## [Let not my love be call'd idolatry,]

lacybottomed (all violently red)—
doewoman bones lavishly, rod
deep in moss / lilac's gayness—break nail
—sensual hole / soot / tendon—fir cove
(tidy storm nook)—dry womanlike void—
untie clot snarl—neon sex acts—cowl lined
in cotton—ferns reach for eyes / covet my den—
flog scene / fox hunt—deer straining—pee sieve
(tank filled)—rim a star ring (yum)—a nude
horn—savor dried fruit—gnaw day knottier—
snip man tendon, vanish, hinge—set city in
cup (fewer horses)—hand hides crow's foot—i *them* (neon,
fat, horned, veined)—elk id—*fear*: an oval unit (
iron, tin)—pee event: well chokes with anther.


## [When in the chronicle of wasted time]

moonswitch twitch (a deer)—i he / fennel
frond—*he, she, i* stratifies, twigs to pieces—
i feud *you: manly, male*—breathtaking bud
(dank delight)—divine day: sea / pool; i fernlass;
the boys blaze / bone; he-unit wets, fattens;
i dew off—*bony*: of hooffoot, of pearl
hue—a tit vein—a sexdripped, queer wholeness—
uneven you touch beast, sway—a smear
or euphoric rite—shear pelt (is passable
faun)—oyster rim—lip tough fig, oil, rue—
i get toy—tidy bush / naked horn—divine wolf
howls in the hour—gut stag kindly—root, honey,
brew—chew hyphenations—dew held forest so—
tie goat—round rune / code: two shapely baskets.

## [Not mine own fears nor the prophetic soul]

cup neon fist—hornier women shatter pool
with gore, moonlight, a moon—fir scent wedded
to clean fur, holy cove—rye, nettle, oats—*me*,
perfect as food / soot—i pondfoam undies—
her strap-on (horned, hilted)—oh, cute male-me,
die (a sharp gouge, a chasm)—tusk worn tender—
sweetish dusts (clove, cinnamon)—i warren / steer—
ovalgendered (a palace / co-op)—flimsinesses
of waspish thorn—i, mostly wet, dim the tomb—
butch tells me i'm a dyke (fresh sobs)—vase (no odor,
no thin, lily rot)—chemise oversimplifies hip,
reduces to lethal, blue lisp (sewless)—hind shrine
on the mountain—hunt hymn's filth, adds it
to nectar, herb stems, pansyfrost, swanbend, stars.


## [What's in the brain that Ink may character]

tame hart / hyacinth twinkier—a branch sat
at the root—citrus perfuming the hide—hit (why;
sweetness)—i thaw *knot* to *hag, raw pewter,*
*rhyme* (a rye harvest)—am told i'm sex pottery—
work bussy, eat it—honeying rib—*pelt* yet *veined*—
he yeses at hysto—i am marecurve / day
light (cotton, unheeding moon hunt)—*i* in idol—
wolf eats fawn, hind, hare (slim hairy event)—
oval she-altar, feverish stone—colt seen
standing—i fed estuary—oh, gownjut / he
-stick, sing perversely—neonsore, a claw
opens—if *bra, tit—i*: gay kumquat—hey, sea
god, hold, rest—i invite tonic effect (herb, fern,
mushroom tea)—waded (low tide)—we rift houndward.

## [O never say that I was false of heart,]

feel veinwreath of a throat—say *ass*,
say it—cam queen buffs gem—oh alloyed *them*—
*imagery* palms *history*—deem staff
frothy (silicone)—bath: mostly hes, raw, humid—
a shaven dome—oh, themfog, veil it *fairy*—
marring leather, haunt it—visit lake
to watch it extend, hum, hem—teethe joint gist
(tasty bone)—fragrant moss, firmly hew it—
*nude* (merely no tee)—hunger hive vibrating
labial fold—i asked her to flog balls—entities:
body / chest (a proportion)—idle lusts (statue
of fag idol)—oath omen: gust / lovely thorn—
florid caving (the lush noise)—i winter—
you *hi* tartly—i halve monstrous meat.


## [Alas, 'tis true I have gone here and there,]

ate night to see river (a hare unleashed)—
vanity of meadow heat—melt, yes, meld
(mead's smooth gold etch)—ripe organ wets hunt—*i*: shadow
of woman scent—see off dance of field—
i root, hart, violet, dust—mouth at the skin—
boy (tan, lank)—salt, sage, candy—a verb, blue
as meat—gather the sleeve—horny honeybutch
bosses me, *nose the velvet*—a fad: powdery, rosy
hollowness—wanted vanilla head—oh haven /
ripe rim, penetrate me—no wild veiling,
only tender fern—if porn, doe to arrow
moon with dildo—enfoaming a cove—
comb, weave, hem textile—gent-envy them-sheen—
men moan (perverts)—vanity blots out the gods.

## [O for my sake do you with Fortune chide,]

woody chemistry of *tea*—i unhooked fur
(dog god rhyme)—shestud fumed—lily feast,
a deft rend / mottled rib—oh to verify tip /
rub pulse—bind, cinch, enchant (warm blasphemies)
—i harvest ache—see my mint / nectar combed neat—
lure / ambush at tendons—my cute dandies
whir elknaked—thyroid thins to sweat
(wipes wet rind)—ewe / hind, a net rhyme—
periwinkle twinkling, dahlia slit—will it
soften one (yes)—i sing moist clotting for pain,
bitten breast, thistle (*whorl* knit in it)—
to crone crone crone (reproducible)—*no tact*
defines me—a dire hurt, a pansy—tiny deer
tan the eve—i mouthe your oystering cup.


## [Your love and pity doth the impression fill]

hounds stir the rye field—i ply oval moon tip,
oval plumtang—cub paws chin—my hard words
wolf hollow—relish lilac, cream, water
(loamedged)—boywool, young rosemary,
mead—i trans lush—your overtly wild meat,
red, open—an arrow says, *hunt*—to moosemusk my fig,
oil it—neon elevator semen (no one
here)—stan stag legs, thin, rhymed—*corset* or *gown*,
wonderful sophistry—a bloom, a cairn,
a hot mess—dry fetish (carves stone doe
to eat lard)—tarot's perfect prediction:
tower, lion, death—gems nymphdick—i sew
on eyes, ply moods—rapturous berrying—
skeletal deer—motherliness with bad, dad hat.

## [Since I left you, mine eye is in my mind,]

i *me* cutely—i synonym—i feminineside—
hecate's goth dog—hunt vibrato / *woman*
*pitch*—rind lands in dirt—fan at holy subtop
(guts me ineffectually)—so bees use it,
froth it, tend a hole—*i'm* rots forever—
hold hoof, hips, flood (witchcraft)—i water herb
in pot—jade themhorn / bitchshaft—so quick
to show crotch (validations)—how hind thins—
tie steeds (foresight, their fluttersong)—
frostmuttered surface—remove head's wet root
(sanguine toothrot)—a dirty hem—heathen
rite (feathery cuts)—wove sore mouth heat—droop
of opulent pear—i'm a boychewer—i let
them taste it, my neon ruin / musky deer museum.


## [Or whether doth my mind, being crown'd with you,]

gown tribute / dim, rhythmic drown—oh honeydew,
fragrant hemp, hyacinth tusk—our idle pelts'
amateurish lather—i witness her holy eye
close—thud that hit ovary (animal gut)—they
sing foammess song (tend it)—i knot / thread
runes (*beech* issues fable)—her wet, curly moss—
crave decrypting *babe*—fetter sea
to ebb fetish—amasses ass—a closet's jamb
terrifies—hesitantly tiny fists—to gem /
to gild my untidy kinkdrip—smart men sang,
(lush times)—twigs withering—one hewn ewe—gay silk
chaps (rip)—pouted, atop heath, antlered
hind—*i* is seen bottle, is soft spire—
oh, heart, tendon, tit, be deviling—satisfy me.

## [Those lines that I before have writ do lie,]

erosive tide: i beast thin, featherhollow—
deer hovers aesthetically out on dune—oat void /
horny, honey game—my junk went wet—tends
studflower—a reblunted slur / clam, a fleshy form (arm,
anus, billowing corns)—tied men—cocked, i tit / hem—
sex infected (again)—chew words pink—grove scent,
snatch taste, planetary rib hunt—tensest bud
forms to girth (round attentiveness)—i retch gold / sing
foam—sinewy hag antler—tiny frays
in the weave—tiny boyish moons—to glut,
to intertwine—weary i cinch a snare—
cute porn—snow on the bridge—tightest fern
shoot beneath moss—a baying (veil it
violet)—wolfthigh twitch—hart (lost, goldwrought).

## [Let me not to the marriage of true minds]

tongue / rim a soft hole—tender meat trim—
mind leitmotiv (doe, moss, petal, vein,
hart, hilt, waist, fawn)—incoherent slide
(strewn rib)—hooved mother—move tree
to invoke sex—a dim refrain:
eat harvest, smoke, stones, pond—thin ankles
vinetwist—artery rite (beargod shank)—
night enshawls house—hook / web goth twink—hare hunt
unfolds (smooth rope choke)—i hag sly, sent violets
in these hips—moon climbs neck, swigs acid
(she blushes)—war horse in a field—work it to vent—
tug me soft, devour it—to bone, be doeheat /
doehue—trans vibe: *i'd perform porn*—
riven nerve, red oval, winter moon.

## [Accuse me thus, that I have scanted all]

mulch, tactile, devastates—a seahunch
(water's rude hypnosis)—eerie or daughterly
scoop—even out fur, lay leg, drool—tarot
yawned at me—*heredity* bold as bloody
fawn / bearhewn hive—neonknit squint—thud met
thigh (*more, again, now*)—cove, taper, turn—druid dyes
it in thistle tea—dovetail hold—wash ash
off pants—i'm trash orchidslur—shout wet gore rhythm
(no fury woe)—mold breasts—work blond shin
fur—sour cup / stem juice—*almond* as *a not*
*-berry*—howl hint: untie wolf—*grove* if men
stay in town—a mouth honed to true beak
(divine carve)—pale roots' mess—i spy pit (day
heat's only furry nova)—i doe / cuntcovet.


## [Like as to make our appetites more keen]

no tree—i eat reek (peat / musk / loam)—i spoke
so opalurge (cup wet hunger)—i tear *meadow*
into *nature*—lend us a map so severe—
new scenes (in strips): go suck hunk / hew ewe—
fig sweetens if burnt, conveys gore—you feel neon
foam / mist—tree budding fat eyes—i cried—
fawns smokedrunk in a field—feces (a soft node,
eerie, dead)—the edges thin to water—beastrunes
(i notch stone)—i, a poet, put *ivy, lilac,*
*throat, tide*—swells wet at hornluster—use *fag*
as name, feel butch elation—a tight rod thud
(a bowl rings)—we fucked so boredly—idolhunch
in bone hunt—tans deer (leather scent)—fluid
root of *i*—am hips / cud / us—oh elk, sing softly.

## [What potions have I drunk of Siren tears]

a pink hurt—a wet fern—hair nests so ovoid—
do fold / cull fetishhankies—slim limb twirl
fades—she pegs a top (pansy porn)—i froth aloe,
wilting wolfishness (its lonely maw)—
hare tether twitch—domed warmth—scar to rhyme
the healing—i've lush thirsts—soft blot shed wet
poem—boy's reined fetish—to see we unearth hive heft /
gender as *disc, fat hind, moon tit, hive rift,*
*fire fit*—full, i tendon / bone—ow (i
bite tit [bit badly])—reverse stealth (melt)
—lunation is bled uneven—i withdraw
into former star swagger—aster ring for hart after
rut or tend—boycott men / seek ruin—
snag (hare in hand)—etch violet petal in my rib.


## [That you were once unkind befriends me now,]

knifewound woe—manbody hecunt—tree resin
in hair (the scent)—odd flow of hardwither /
mysterious mounds—new breasting rends
(unrested)—yes, nerves swarm—amber horsesmell
/ boyish winefunk—naked, furry, messy one—
heavy symbol for *sea*—i lay out, used, sip
on tea—a vale hides a turn: yearn knit
to woodier worm—if i churn i gush—eye fence;
get over it—hewn he-humid bottom—hag (forearm
/ wrist deep, washed out, sore)—horn sets rhyme—
sound oystered to taunt a honeyed moon—
hunt / disembowel wolf—some shaved-bush itch (
wears booty shorts)—*beef* as cute meat pun—
moss, rosemary, modernity—sun mourns (am a sun).

## ['Tis better to be vile than vile esteem'd,]

bled violent theme (tie testes, vibrate,
probe, observe)—he, erect in gown (into chafe)—
deerhush meets dawn's cool pelt—i adjust *his*
to *theirs*—boy bulge softening—burn *eye*
(the letter for)—house's dreadful holysea sway—
opt to boyvisual, to administer glove
for fist (wearily impersonal)—hairy seer
scattering wild batch—i hunt how i hold kin—how i
halve *them*—tiny dahlia tat to name
the rune—i am raw, open—stocky sub
begs to hurt (i hate this game)—shyly be velvet hem, be
button—we, hounds both, trek—my draghem synthesis
(a veil, a litheness)—tiny, trans hinge—mule
gnarled in barn—*be* eats *i*—*name* held as rind.


## [Thy gift, thy tables, are within my brain]

stag rib femininity—*he* tartly (why: bath
house witchcraft)—trimly land ram leg
(thin as meat)—a whole river, hill, hand, back
(tender body eaten neatly)—violet
string / antler as taboo—had ornate leash
fantasy—i butter / butch so suavely—
a horned bear (i'll top)—idolize salt, ivy itch
shedomes, carved bone—try finer etch (
tool held to cup)—touch moon, torn, tarnished,
sore—tie doe tails—*valley*: northern code
for *door*—i wet them-meat firm—he begs love,
*cover mouth*—teethes so—taste bitter, leather
boot—men permeate *tree*—detach junk,
moisten it—furl to green forms, weep.

[61]

## [No! Time, thou shalt not boast that I do change,]

i touch tablet as oath—night's anon method: to
bury plumwidth in wet earth—my hipgist /
themtang—slit neon, nova, horn (engorge it)—
fag ass / rosebud—girthfroth me—tiny seer,
a soft bee ode—raw-eared fire rune—third mare
is lush stud—tuft oath in woods—a hot top
broken—a round, hermitmother—a sad tree
(heathen oak)—do them—vertebral theft / thaw—hind
theory: edge fetish, a thirsty bend—
tighten horse tendon (snap)—no wetter trap
(eel / wren)—dew's hydrostatic fatherhood—
a honed bone symmetry—illustrate chaos:
do shave raw—do veil—thin belt hiss—
wild theyhunt: be the deer (i pelt, i ecstasy).


## [If my dear love were but the child of state,]

be my watercolor hush—*i* deviates (felt deft)—
a thorn throbs—a terf fumes—i'd dab fern, gut it
sore / smooth it—metal object (stave)—tie us
to free the sea / field—gown glows warm / red—sword hews
me wet; unbinds cord—i of radical fat—
softs floral finger in plump moss, in tin
(held, unfolded, bent)—witch (antler, roots,
flint)—hormones touching—i salivate, i wet her
lips—hecate at forty (thin, erotic)—
*cunt* or *bush*—horse skids / hoof—seen: warm whorl—
he in pelt, a stagboy, all sun cult idol—
hand torn with writhing—*sweat* so *shower*—throw rot
as cloth—*fetish* is *motif* (soil, welt, tone)—
void-fed hornforms—i dew, echo girlish, hew a cove.

## [Were't aught to me I bore the canopy,]

pewter *i* to *cage*—boymouth / earthen
urn—worrying hot hound meat—i hew text
(stone for readability); *regret* as
harsh moonrune—hair's winter growth—cove / pit
fur—floweriness, a vernal omen—to dovehand
manly god born, metaphorically, out / seen
in stag form—rouge floods cup—*snip* (wove more
gush)—i zing in ripe filthtaint—perverts,
unquestionably—see bitter he-homo
eat boy trouble—to pour thin, naked foam
in sexnotch, wish on twist (sword / dick)—oh *man*,
unfortunate mode—try *her* / *elm* / *blue*
*comfort*—bear hurts doe—*i*: one lush unrune /
mint-laced nettles—my pond has cost (throw ash in).


## [O thou, my lovely boy, who in thy power]

you *they* my hip (bowlenvy)—oh wool rot,
oh smoke—glides so rich / licks the salt fluids—
nightgown waist sewn to hone—drawn by harsh
wrists, thighs, glow—eat wet, nervy oyster flesh
(a soft mass)—i rivercurve—i work green nets—
i sap—eat hollow skull on stalk—screwed tight cub
(asterisk holes)—spike teeth—the lush prophet,
his little neck—arm in deer gut's maw (dim decay)—
hue of opal, of hare horns—i tie my tree rune
(neat-eyed ruin)—*lust*: elk's hot breath / ripe steam
hued the light—raw mound—a seedy stud bar—
desire's equine-throated hunter.

## [In the old age black was not counted fair,]

a hag / doe cock (fasten it on)—i blur and welt—
*i*, a soft ewe / bitter binary omen—rue to
ease bones / tissue—buck's ivy crawl—i butch
husbandly—wash mane / read birds (at [date], at
sunrise)—open a hand: a feather, crotch, powhunt—
*roughed*: how to flail, rein, staff—rawest fabric
worn, wet, blue—am honeyoath / honeybeast,
*doubling* as rift—*ass*: divine perfection—
froths (semen, cove, strawberries)—am lyre / bark
(sound sat eerie)—horse eyes my tender mush—
buck aura flowers hyacinth—*tan, no boot,*
*into ice*—leaf's sagittal sheen—new, red ram
brought to the moon ceremony—yes, i *we* if
you knot a hurtoval—they used *boy* to see glass.


## [How oft, when thou, my music, music play'st,]

mouth as smutcup / mythic wolf noise—why
(to sweeten)—pond blooms hind—oh woo us as stud
with theystag swing—we tensely hunt frosty hew /
dirty neon—chain wound to catch—seerform
sees limp dahlia bent janky—covet hot
hit / rend / thaw—softhorned deity sank,
whipworshiped—poolarc / hillmyth that harvests us
(the beastly bent)—dawn's dishonest bloodgush—
i stroke cuntache (total delight)—sweet he-body,
hide and hip—thin cut, a wincing—*to toss*, as
in *hair*—work wet shaft tightly—gownglee me
with gelding—too vanilla—am bred / pinked—moss
in cushy ease / a jockstrap—*i* as in *psych*—
kiss thirsty he-hem / empty fisting glove.

## [The expense of spirit in a waste of shame]

effeminate top's sheswish—pain eater—ox
cult—salt slut—tin talon / incision aid—
your perfume (jade moss, field, bull blur)—*door*
or *rectum* or *sleeve*—a stag rut / nude text—
joints bound sore—spaded the oystering—
pat ass (adore sound)—a hen / tendon / horn—
in beast, a raw opal thawed (salad toss)—
pear's kindhearted meat, plum too—oak
is poisonspun—i'd dress as mountain
gods (thin, requiem, and vex)—heat at haven
wood (bind, lap, veinsap, or a rosy fever)—
peep doe bra—*form* joins body, head, ear
into lewd whole / shell—stark new snow—knelt lowly,
attentive, heathen—*let's slash*—oh hold / hunt me.

## [My mistress' eyes are nothing like the sun,]

transmisogynists seek hymen lie / "true" *he*
of her (methodical rip)—rare, red snarls
(boyish hair)—sew wet hernest—the fawn burned
(forehead aglow)—hew sinew, ribs, herb, iris—rack
(shed winterdead horns)—i evade seam, ask
crush to hush (*be creeknoises*)—seen,
hunter deems doegore ripe filth—miss-name
me (thinnest break / froth)—meaty thrash stirs me—
we heal horse ankle, wive elk, pity root
at high moon phase—cum-salted fur—a strain
in weaving—doe rode stag—grass
grew monstrous and kind—amethyst hews her less
than ivy—oh leaky, needy men—a starverib—
my *she* peels, watches a boar in a field.

## [Thou art as tyrannous, so as thou art,]

*to rut* as horny status—oath or sauna
smoke (cruel shape)—they disembowel a suture oath
/ dahlia form—oh knotty welt / sweet ground rot—
a lush hare / soft comet—we tear up tired joints
bent too fast—hide / sheathe hay deity gloom
(new moon chafe)—to eat hart, glyph throat / evoke
it—heat stones—red boyrear bloody—
steal laurels then hoof it—gay, i mow
in torn shorts—fable: situate a sad ewe
on rug—a hot thigh unbent—a faint sky (do a scan:
no odes)—neon rhinestone backwaters—
spy three majestic dicks—flaunt big, manly
tits—a hound breathing on neck—i'd *he* vastly,
eat seed, naked, crotchless in harthind spin.


## [Thine eyes I love, and they, as pitying me,]

divine hyphenate stag—i eye silty omen—
twink / twigthin homo shard—easy, tender mint
leaves—a cuntpink, lamb horn (bound)—grove /
tiny, plum pit—working a hurt, honey pot—
transmoon hunghunt / ovary tide—fennel,
/ beets (hot heft)—she goes back—cemetery tree
feverlathers—that horsethin ulna stunt
(try hot shethrob)—saw tall god of teeth
eye me in gay bar—touch of wet moss—see notch
meat heat relentlessly—hew / tie both—
ring fern to echo geometric starhum / nude moon—
tie ivy—ply key—pear's thin, taut rind /
sweet rib—full waterlily shine—bask (*ache*
to *cake*)—count pill total—halfhymn ladyhex.

## [Beshrew that heart that makes my heart to groan]

gather matter to make breasts—thaw horny heath—
my vasetuft, hidden, tended, roaming—if *power*
then *outlet* or *go to mountain seer*—
fist's sweet, round salt—be my velvety bearsmut—
frothy he-arm cult—seek fat elm (eye hymn
to the dead)—flex arms, grunt, harden shy sons—
he smears a milky omen—*f-off*—ate hind
butchered in forest—smoothes cloth (tart, red
berry on it)—womanly spit streams—oh shed
form (entrans it)—they boyblur—tamed leather hip—
blue theystag whimpered—remake *he* rose—
oh hunter on city moon, tangle its sugar—
now i feather epithet—untidy boneglint /
hilt sham—maidenantler (a perfection).


## [So now I have confess'd that he is thine,]

*woven*: hide / shone—taste chaos in shift
(nightgod flies away)—melt my tar / mold—
lift feet, tie him, horny, aloft—morsels,
clot, rot—he lusters to rim wifely bottom,
to holehunt, to winterwolf—i, bent bluer,
ask (nods no)—curvature (hoof, tit, hide)—
rude ewe feels hairy—milk torn to butter,
hand bound to hand—dab at thirst / fist them
(they slow, they bite)—oaktuft (taut), *he* (taut)
roots (taut)—lush petalhurt—stout he-fur—
i do aftercare, dry naked sub foam (semen)—
luminous gush thins—i he-mark doeboy,
thistle him—a shamebath (oh hound vomit)—
a "new" halftype—horse meat (honeyed it).

## [Whoever hath her wish, thou hast thy *Will*,]

oh hart with holly, with severe thawhush
loll—lewd vibration / pulsation (down
there)—an all-homo taunt—thigh (time vexes
it)—hesitantly woodsmanlike (gut width /
urinal heswag)—sea is wooldull—i top switch—
i etch hillsoft doe in coin—unwoven, my heat
hum lessens—woollier staggirl hair itch—
pendants (in a cairn)—i feel womanly / chic
(tie eerie veil)—trans, a hart calls sweetly—
union (drenched, stoned)—data as habit
(gather, stow)—i hunt hindcowl / lily libido—
working metal ore into wheel—mollify *male*,
its neon flicker (lean, brushlike, done)—
alone, i thaw, melt, unlink handbone, tilt.


## [If thy soul cheque thee that I come so near,]

quietly cute themache—horse hoof is neat
width / turn—sea thaws hollowly, a bit silty
and shallow—i work nude thistle, tidy stem—
sweet fat, fur, velum—lily hoists off velour
suit / her wetly full hall—wolf, violet, fire
swallowed (awful, tinny film)—i lilt hilly,
peg raw with vers perfection—i hinge to tease—
neon omen: an ermine sang buckodor
to nimble the plumhunt—neaten dress—
butch hysterics (not *too* tough)—i am unseen /
stareflooded—the smooth hip / long he-line—
teeth (stamen) teeth—moon's hot weightgain—
am a velvet bull (its dank, loamy tone)—the myth
wove transly, hummed hill to intense foam.

## [Thou blind fool Love, what dost thou to mine eyes,]

to houndboy, half-veiled, to thistlewomen—so *out*
they stealth the tone—honey's thawed bead
in his ear—boyishly we wet the ewe tusk, eat,
stew weak, horse teeth—hot, tasty tit ebb
/ tipcloy—porous ivory break—felt ears
were deercloth—enanimal hehair / bend by
gay's soft froth—oh fake-eyed does—oh woolhush,
your wet heft—*get me meds*—hart joint / hide /
husk—rawly held my petalthin throat to shave—
manhole warmth slows cockwidth—new hypodermic
rite (eyes thigh omens)—sits in noisy sea
of fur or fat—lacehunt—top us, utopia,
shatter us hard and green—i rhymering yet thieve—
oh torn, pagan star—deer fat furled sweetly in ash.

## [When my love swears that she is made of truth,]

wove he-swath softer—deem as *thirst* / humanly
wet—unhook higher beehives—idols lie
on their stone thighs—mouthhum at dyke mutt
(wears tail in bed, nestled, unhurt)—feel loss
as gush / sinkhole—i knit my night, envy that hunt
god's warm boyshape—test the yank's lush heat,
identify lines, prep gag ritual (chokemess)—
stud pushes up dress (thirstsop, nimble hoist,
joyous, heathen fur)—sun sets, i stew herbs
into tea—am a dry wheat field—*horn* so
*bite*—to trans *bulge*, moss it—*she* is vein
to *vase* or *seen*—oval (gold, heavy)—tail, tendon,
hide—heflower's winter heat—i hem *their*
to fit salty bear—fed, a bull rune widens.

## [O call not me to justify the wrong]

cuts wolf leg at joint—try *he / moon*
/ *nylon net*—musky pit hunt—hare sat shady
in the wood—honey gut, numb with wet teeth—unity
in watery boyness—plow earth raw / put dome
in mouth—thirsty glove—sweet melt—blue heels—
a fabric-eared doe, her antler—seethe gay into
gownthaw—hunt hung switch / dom—the unhewn identity
opens me—nethermoss scenery—if added, a rib
cloys the skeleton—we hem wave / luxe elm—
break severe moon theism—they peel nine
chrysanthemums (a freer form)—fed on soft eye
/ sweet, mushy date—i tether here (jarring hilt hit)—
botanical monstrosity—ennui eased
(hardly)—horse (i gut it)—milk manwood til pink.


## [Be wise as thou art cruel, do not press]

sew a copse rune—bestial odor / thrust—
i dote on man's cunt (huge, timid peach)—i tow deity
down to expanse—sword's smell / sword's red err—
whine, tiny, porny fagment, pant—i am
bitter witch (*fight me*)—tie / tire eweheat—
to melt, to song, you tool the velvet hole—
tense *he* waters thin, mystic break—enshade
without manness—pink theyfoal, chew rib / horns—
i warp *druid* lush for me—god of soil hid as
field, as stone, as empty hand—milking hem
(gownbillow)—drowning horse (its wild stars)—
beard bedevils, dreamy mane—slab (deer's
ribs, moonlit, honed)—eat beauty hot
as you do a bright hurt—dewing hot e-they—*steer, pear, thigh.*

## [In faith I do not love thee with mine eyes,]

i home teeth naively—the infinite woods
house the tan doe—ornate horns terrify
/ devastate him to stay—they brush white pelts
dissatisfied—hole devotion (we weep)—top
ghosts me on grindr—i wet *he*-id—unnatural eyeteeth
perforate linen sheets—bone (gruntcooed
in restroom, nervebodied as nettleslit)—
*i* (seen as fleshy whole)—to taunt a neat
curve—my sensitive fawn moss—feint by
shading—is horsehair fur—feed tote love's omen
(thin, ode volume)—skew halfway (a saneness
destroys, heaved)—a hart vow—lapels (butch / trans)—
lush, gay malfunction—i may gut no prey—
i tame weak hands, manmeat, thirstshapes.


## [Love is my sin, and thy dear virtue hate,]

vivid rite—a honeyed slur—an amethyst
moon set in gold—ivy, fur / fang us—lone hind
in winter's mouth (a pit)—touch the bow—eat omen
to avoid it—thorn rune / fresh, dim plant sting—
i dot noon—i smother—soft ripe of *filth*,
of *peachlather*—met trans otter as hind, raven,
flat maidenfade—foal noses ovals so, bends
redder—bone's feverish throb—true sob nest—
situate velvet leash—silhouette: bowl, hoof,
the moon's neon eyehum—tie / wait / whip me sore
(tit wept)—thaw horny night hysteria—root,
body, empty heap—tree ivy, its tide /
twist—teahouse thud fetish—oh hot ode / vodka
shot—am blue nab / ply sex—deity, feed me.

## [Lo, as a careful housewife runs to catch]

a flower, a curl, a futchness, too—i us-ache,
broken as water—doe fur, hare fat, ocher eye—
hind dawnshakes, foams, wets bed—can bite strap
(told to)—heavy trans gushhunt—i use wifehip
to drench clit—shell hid geldache—hews shrine /
chest—burns sweet herbs—archaic, i coyote
(eat the offal)—i scorch the bell—we of whir, of
pert, trans shit—pond notion: frozen, icing
(that sweet shit)—if soft half-rut, no horn—cure hem—
heathen, i scythe wheat / hair (ebbs if bald)—
thick butch booty (cup fat)—mutate he-horn,
bend it—mark pelt / doe's pink ass—myth: hare
with my paw, holly, salt—i heavy, i throatlust—
blush at my ordinary clitdick, fount, lung.


## [Two loves I have of comfort and despair,]

fed strap-on as woodheft—i rim oval cove—
silk's slight twilight—i wrote / cup messode—
grab hair, tighten fist—am lean tree—
i do iron lust / worship (coral,water, elm
omen)—fem ovation—see hem lilt lowly,
tease men—met rot—met my deft ribglyph /
raw ivy—bent moon ritual (coats puddled
on floor)—i rupture dish—i whip / theywig—
why tend tender fragment—be dahliahunt—
melt lead / lust—tiny, cryptic sub, *toe
firm on tongue*—the charm ebbed—bit of both
(horn / hen)—sage essential oil—lunge
(the elk hunter)—bit any wound violet—i bliss
meaty—gold god rune—bone lily, foam it.

## [Those lips that Love's own hand did make]

homo spit stoked the vanilla dew—hands
feather the dead (hot thudhits)—boarstain
(guts' heat)—am skirthole / hornfade—
mount sweaty sub—hew halfsweet
deer theism—i tighten my orchard arc,
weave it—cut the stone—get nighthard—
unwinds gloving image to seed
gut—round, titsag heat, then a wet
sweatline—had heathen dirt,
nailedged—thaw (totally soft)—
gowntwinkle filthhole—i add hoof
(a hollow hetone)—my leafshiver / fawn
-hair—they saw the water foam—
deify moonstag—say *nude* vainly.


## [Poor soul, the centre of my sinful earth,]

felt ceremonious froth push ornately
(*there*)—horseplay—brew the aster tea
for pain—studheft stun—honey raw hidewidth—
i wand ass / tang you—thirsty polyglot claw,
*encore*—glossy goth swath—lavish area so
it pumps fountains—song dyed on hand—hot
ass / exthirst—relic: some wolfish horns
dyed *oh* / chantruby—tipsy i hag, test *she*,
nerve voluptuously—ash lost hot thinness—
tip the tender staghole—tag a ratty nova
on ig (*THIS*)—you find river, moss, bull, redness
intertwined—firm butch, *hi*—oh bee, woo
fundamental softness—oh death, oh doe teeth
edge me—chat as i tend daddy on her neon throne.

## [My love is as a fever, longing still]

glassgleam on velvet—only *sir* if i
consent, asshole—a red thighwrithe—the fur
coat, shelved, fingered—whittle the horn / hip
petite—i tint shakespeare conceptually
(ha, see that)—i rim cove—poly synonym:
open to thirst—he-pink scarring (a tapestry
trans formational)—he peeped wave depth,
witchshade ciphersex—they did ice dips—
arrowspit—cute as nip—omen: a seascar
cavern—warm fruitsmother—did neaten
seam mess / chrysanthemum god ruin—sad: today,
this month or year—vex standard terf—plum
stone hid gene orb—whiff that trough (hartheavier
stagstank)—lick ash raw—bled a halorash.


## [O me! what eyes hath love put in my head,]

swampymouthed they heave—loinheat /
harsh cunting—widen cove—echo tetherworship
of theyjugs—held fawn / river deity—hem me
higher—sulfate scent / leather taste—why say
*i* or *my sweet heft*—i feed leafy beast a horn,
a wreath, a holy stone—mist tints woods
to violet blot—tend hewn hole—fit *need*
in my ass, let out alone (love soreness)—
*wine? yeah* (use nectar bowl)—oh to cove
this sex, withdraw it—notch shave—dig at want
like a worm—i mouth *them*—envy hive's tang,
its vernal clot—fetish: lean hunt—sees eels
in pond—eat butch musk / lose ewe—night (torn veil)—
i lush fistlunged (fleshy, wooden, salty)—let us flee.

## [Canst thou, O cruel, say I love thee not,]

hothouse rot—a lacy, violet cunt (seen
late at night)—wipe mess with hanky—a free
gin drink / tote—whitehot neon hoof
rattles (shaken)—my form: alloy, taffy,
waterthin mold—oh hatchet a theyfield—
oh hunt soft nut (womanwood froth in paw,
fur, tendons, hip)—*i*: tool / unsteady moon /
ravenous glyph—twin omens: ferment / pee
tint (hydrate)—mimic flowers' seep
/ strive—do up pit esthetics (yes, odor has
lewd comfort, that dewy bliss)—*the hyphen*
as embodiment—citymoon heft—honeyed
toy—knit / wove flab, hormone, thin wound
into this unsolvable chest—am hand, doe, teat.


## [O from what pow'r hast thou this powerful might,]

top's warm mouth, hip, thigh, fur—wet floweroath so
it eats coineasy—why cuff him (wintry
gutglee)—i rim / taste them—he took me, ivy
-haired, staggowned—chatty otter's tan hand—herbs'
long infusion—wash thigh, chest, tit, heel—comb
hurt's feathery heftnest—voideyed,
i flush red—tore green chintz—shank (its raw salt)—
sword bent at hilt—i extend my chest, am sly
homowheel—to tug, to heave, to remake: hew them—
feet ache (adjust there)—harmonious ease
(high, bluer throatoath)—wood hooves'
ostentatious thud—wool's heat / throb's rhythm—
seminude transwhir (festive *i*)—holy no
more—to be boy, wet over hedoe filth.

## [Love is too young to know what conscience is,]

you sent violets—choke at iconic gownswoon—
scene on brooch: wolf, vinetwist, skycoo, neon
tree—glam me erotic, gayness, then hunt
me—softly love shy tuft / ugly pelt sea—wets fir
tree—body: i reformat boyunit, hag
*ass* to *oyster* (ploy)—bend norms: bogmartyr
myth, moth myth—a bulleyed lad (toy so
he froths)—moon shifts sea (a vernal turn)—i yelp
(tang in mouth)—thin to a deer hip (yet to bust)—
top is rindrip / frothsip—humid pasturehaze—
butch deity dons rod to peg—note: here
is shaft and base (lily)—dry off that tiny
notch—lilac theist—canine claw—too fond
of her—fold sore hide lovelier (a velar swan).

## [In loving thee thou know'st I am forsworn,]

unweave silk with thorns—no figrot moon
(restorative glitch of *new*)—women bust out arrow,
bow, knife (dianabent)—hot, nervy wattchord
wavelength—we gnaw on raven bone—if i tire,
brew tea—coy hood oath (the cub's wet, fuchsia
bud)—he enjoys tit tweak—warm men riper
with mouth (marvelous feast)—a lobe oysters
insistently—moth (fleshtone)—a dahlia
nova—offer eyeshards to deep pond, sink the wish—
frothy volttoy honesty—cunt's haythatch
hedge (tightness eaten loose)—bind evenly, tan
their hide (*show me*)—generate amethyst as tang—
I am furred hornier—he-jaw or festive rope—
foliage that outlines sour hartsweat.

## [Cupid laid by his brand and fell asleep,]

bleed bull (lip, hair, spine)—sad candy fad—
anon, i shave a dad, dig a staff into mud,
stir daddylevel dick in hole—figpink sequin
froth—an idol (lunate god of ivy, cunt, anal,
riverdoes, holy bitchwolf, form)—oh whir of
illustrative land—oh sedate eyes, tell
nothing, deny map—chew he-twig, ash, vertebrae—
sugaring arc edges, a violet sea—trans (anime
-obsessed, arty, sad)—rim me wifely—event: burnt
bone ritual—subtlety of cherrymood swathed
with kerchief, hide, beads—at hilltops
a teeming depth—triad sheds dust—*i*: a herd
of unfortunate deer—oh my hipbells—butch
fists me cerise—honeysmut grew dewy, ripe.

## [The little Love-God lying once asleep]

i delve elegantly into pool (leg, chest,
hand, hair)—steadily i bind herbs—fangslim, i
felch man (dainty pop)—the myth thaws, skews violet—
mend an empty cup / rib—i, a hind breathing,
tie fat root, fat hip (stroke)—heavy rut
(unwashed hornfroth)—he lays dim water magic—
a seed / grief hole, a short tendon—
raw, vernal singing—his damp daisy bed
(bled on satin)—hequench: hide sly bowlarc—
oh peach heft—to weave: elk us / lip firm rot or
gold—feathering a theyblur (hand, maw,
mesh)—deem mess flirtatiously trans—bird
omen (thrush)—crave pit heat / beard ferocity—
*coves*: to net / overflow—i throw salt (a release)

# Acknowledgments

I would like to thank the editors of the following publications for
including sonnets from this book, in these and earlier forms, in their
pages: *Afternoon Visitor, Annulet, beestung, Bennington Review,
The Brooklyn Rail, Couplet, Changes, The Experiment Will Not Be
Bound: An Experimental Anthology of American Writing, Foglifter,
Fugue, Moist Poetry Journal, Peach Mag, Pigeon Pages, Poetry, The
Puritan, The Recluse,* and *Sporklet.*

I would also like to thank the following:
The Poetry Project and Wayne Koestenbaum for their support
of this project via the Emerge-Surface-Be Fellowship in which I
participated in 2020. This project would never have been possible
without Wayne's good humor, fabulous book recommendations, and
hilariously timed cooking of grains during our Zoom chats.

Justin Phillip Reed, who, after a reading we did together as part
of the Poetry Project fellowship, wrote me and said, "I was thinking
that one of the great freedoms of queerness — and one of its terrifying
quests — is the absence of precedence; indeed, more than rejecting
a set standard, it seems that queering as an act operates beyond /
without a system of standardization. And I think that thwarting a
particular expectation of consumable performance is within that
quest." That was such a source of energy for me as I moved through
these poems. It stuck with me, stuck in me, in my chest. Thank you
for that.

Anselm Berrigan, for being such a generous workshop leader
during my time as a Poets House Emerging Poets Fellow when I
first started this project. I believe you were one of the first to see

any of these poems and, rough as they were, you told me there was something here. I'm very grateful for that.

Sam Ace, and my fellow 2020 Lambda Literary Fellows in Poetry — A.J., Chad, Dolphin, H. Melt, Jesús, Katie Jean, Light, MC, Mimi, Nat, and Tavi — for their generous reading and support of this work. In seeing where you pushed against the work I found what it needed to be. And Lambda Literary (special shout-out to Nicole Shawan Junior), for such a time of intense, queer joy.

Emma Brown Sanders, for giving me the gift of understanding this project and reading a poem from it aloud to me in that shitty apartment. This wouldn't be here without you.

And, as always, to Cormac, for everything, but especially for the special act of care that is knowing how to set the coffeemaker to have coffee ready for when I'd wake up early to tinker with these words.

# Notes

ON THE CONSTRUCTION OF THE TEXT
These poems, what I call "divinations," were created with the
assistance of an online anagramming tool and the source text of
Shakespeare's 154 sonnets. The first line of the corresponding
Shakespearean sonnet is borrowed as the title for each divination.
Using the line as the unit of meaning, the rule I set was to anagram
line-by-line, so each line of the divination has all the same letters as
the corresponding line in the Shakespearean sonnet.

For those interested, here is the URL for the anagramming tool
I used as a kind of virtual Ouija board throughout the writing of
this book: www.wordplays.com/anagrammer/. I later crosschecked
my divinations with Shakespeare's sonnets using www.dcode.fr/
frequency-analysis.

My reference for the sonnets was also online, available through
the MIT newspaper, *The Tech*. See http://shakespeare.mit.edu/
Poetry/sonnets.html/.

Generally, my research for this project included a lot of googling,
but I did have a few books that I returned to over and over as I wrote
these poems whether for informational or lyric inspiration:

*Between Men: English Literature and Male Homosocial Desire* by
    Eve Kosofsky Sedgwick (Columbia University Press, 2015).

*Homosexuality in Renaissance England* by Alan Bray (Columbia
    University Press, 1982).

*Sacred Britannia: The Gods and Rituals of Roman Britain* by
    Miranda Aldhouse-Green (Thames and Hudson , 2018).

*Trimmings* in *Recyclopedia: Trimmings, S\*PeRM\*\*K\*T, and Muse
    & Drudge* by Harryette Mullen (Graywolf Press, 2006).

*Tender Buttons* by Gertrude Stein (City Lights Books, 2014).

This book also has a lineage of form, though I must admit I only learned of these books after I'd started the project — which was a kind of daily ritual to keep me writing during the 2020 and 2021 Covid-19 pandemic and quarantine. Three projects I was pointed to as I shared *The Wild Hunt Divinations* with others were:

*Cunt-Ups* by Dodie Bellamy (Tender Buttons Press, 2018).

K. Silem Mohammad's sonnagrams.

*The Sonnets* by Ted Berrigan (Penguin Books, 2000).

I would also like to acknowledge that the lines "*i was hote shitt*" and "*gendre is not* [  ] *organe*" in "[Tired with all these, for restful death I cry,]" are from Jos Charles's *Feeld* (Milkweed Editions, 2018), the latter of which, in its full form, reads "*gendre is not the tran organe.*"

# About the Author

TREVOR KETNER is the author of *[WHITE]* (University of
Georgia Press, 2021), selected as a winner of the National Poetry
Series by Forrest Gander. They are also the author of three
chapbooks, including *Major Arcana: Minneapolis*, winner of the
Burnside Review award. They have been published in *Poetry*,
The Academy of American Poets' Poem-a-Day, *The Brooklyn
Rail*, *New England Review*, *Ninth Letter*, *West Branch*, *Lambda
Literary*, *Diagram*, *Foglifter*, and elsewhere. A 2020 Lambda Literary
Fellow, they have been a Poets House Emerging Poets Fellow,
an Emerge-Surface-Be Fellow for The Poetry Project, and a
Saltonstall Foundation for the Arts Fellow.